Computer Illusion
in Film & TV

Christopher W. Baker

alpha
books

International Standard Book Number: 1-56761-422-1

Library of Congress Catalog Card Number: 93-73896

96 95 94   8 7 6 5 4 3 2 1

Interpretation of the printing code: the rightmost number of the first series of numbers is the year of the book's printing; the rightmost number of the second series of numbers is the number of the book's printing. For example, a printing code of 94-1 shows that the first printing of the book occurred in 1994.

Printed in the United States of America

Publisher *Marie Butler-Knight*

Managing Editor *Elizabeth Keaffaber*

Product Development Manager *Faithe Wempen*

Development Editor *Seta Frantz*

Production Editor *Michelle Shaw*

Cover Designer *Jay Corpus*

Interior Designer *Barbara Webster*

Layout Designer *Stephanie Gregory*

Production *Gary Adair, Brad Chinn, Kim Cofer, Meshell Dinn, Jennifer Eberhardt, Mark Enochs, Jenny Kucera, Beth Rago, Marc Shecter, Greg Simsic, Kris Simmons, Carol Stamile, Robert Wolf*

Special thanks to Edwin Catmull, Douglas Kay, Carl Rosendahl, and Mike Walsh for ensuring the technical accuracy of this book.

Special acknowledgements

Still from Terminator 2: Judgement Day. *Used with permission of Carolco Pictures Inc. Motion Picture© 1991 Carolco Pictures Inc. (U.S. & Canada), Carolco International N.V. (All other Countries.) All Rights Reserved.*

STRIKING DISTANCE *photographs courtesy of Columbia Pictures.*

Foreword

Hollywood has gone digital, and the old ways are dying. Animation and special effects created with computers have been embraced by television networks, advertisers, and movie studios alike. Film editors, who for decades worked by painstakingly cutting and gluing film segments together, are now sitting in front of computer screens. There, they edit entire features while adding sound that is not only stored digitally, but has also been created and manipulated with computers. Viewers are witnessing the results of all this in the form of stories and experiences that they never dreamed of before.

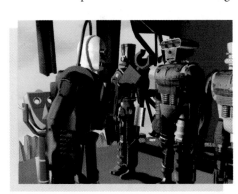

We, in the effects and animation industry today, are in an incredibly unique and fortunate position. Our primary job is to tell stories that entertain, and in the process of doing that, we get the opportunity to work with some of the most creative minds in the world. At the same time, we also have the chance to be leaders and innovators in the visual arts and thus help to push the computer graphics technology forward. In essence, we both sample the future and simultaneously help to define it.

Yet, the progress of the computer technology used in the animation and special effects business tells us more than what the next great film or television show will be. Since our industry demands the maximum performance from both the hardware and the software, we often find ourselves at the leading edge of what is to come for the consumer. For example, from its beginning, the animation and effects industry demanded computers that could display full-color images and full-motion video, accompanied by the capability to integrate and synchronize sound with these images. In addition, we needed to be able to manipulate and render the final look of any 3-dimensional computer image in real time, and to combine the results easily with live-action footage shot on location.

While these seemed like tall demands at the time, virtually all of these early needs are reflected now, not only in the software and hardware we use to create our animations and effects, but also in consumer products that are helping individuals and businesses work, communicate, and entertain themselves. As the communications industry wires our homes with high-speed networks, the need to generate and work with digital imagery will grow ever more important. Beyond home shopping and more compelling games, the evolving digital tools will connect us all more closely together, giving each of us the ability to visualize and interact with people and information from around the world.

Perhaps the most surprising aspect of all this, however, is that the digital effects and animation industry, so well explained and discussed in this book, is still in its infancy. Many of the things we want to do, and know that we could do if the technology were ready, are still out of reach. We dream of being able to do more than just create characters and environments as special effects; we are eager to develop entire stories and experiences from start to finish. We also dream of not simply watching these stories in a passive environment like today's theaters, but of interacting with them directly, of becoming a part of the action itself. These dreams may seem far-fetched today, but they are no more so than the earlier aspirations that have brought us to the present. The technological trends that have carried us this far will continue for decades to come until we have passed the point to which we now aspire and are reaching for the next and even greater vision.

CARL ROSENDAHL
President, Pacific Data Images

Contents

PART II

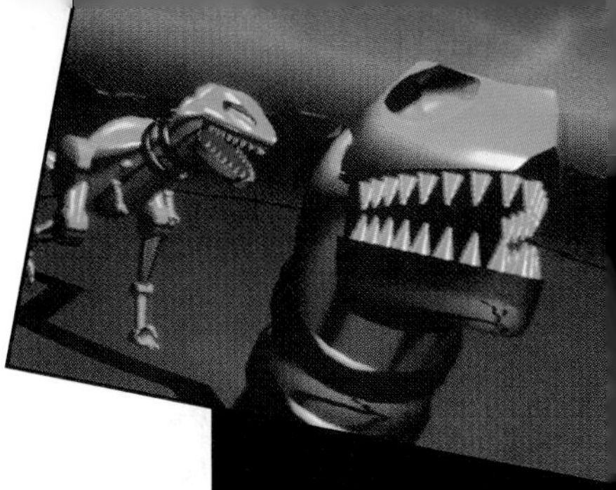

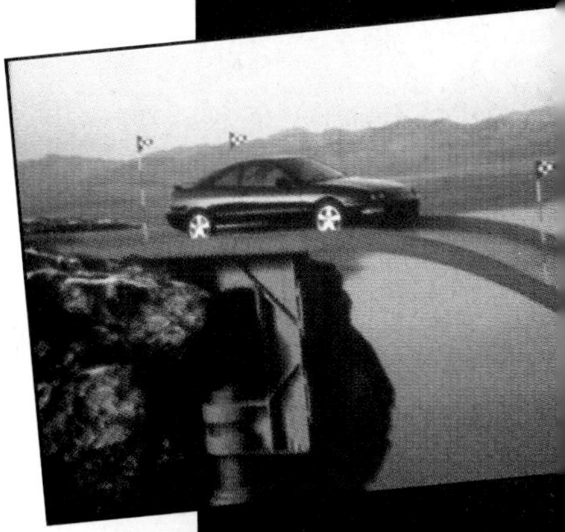

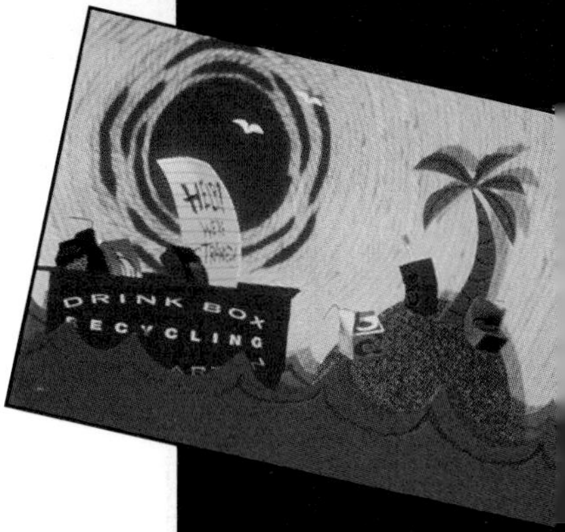
DRINK BOX
RECYCLING

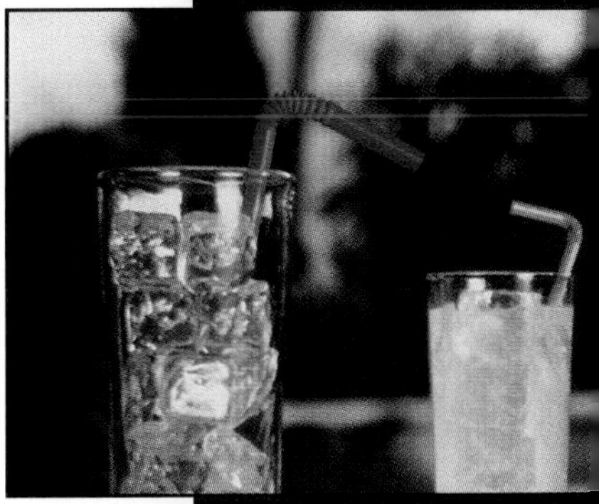

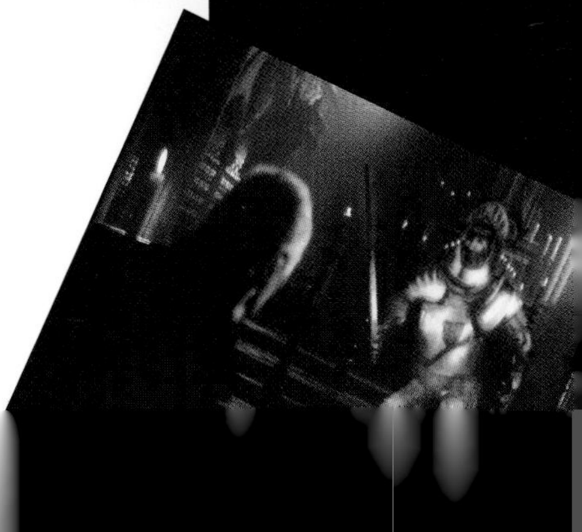

Introduction

I

The velociraptor approaches, hissing and eager, its alien gaze fixed upon its human prey. The humans back deeper into the cavernous entrance hall, torn between meeting the gaze and frantically searching for any escape. A second raptor cuts them off from behind.

The humans watch in terror as their hunter crouches, preparing to spring. The raptor leaps, but is snatched from the air and crushed between the jaws of a raging Tyrannosaurus Rex. The second raptor screams at the foiled attack, and pounces on the Tyrannosaurus, biting and tearing at its flesh. The huge Tyrannosaurus snaps at the second attacker, catching its leg and flinging its body into the remains of the dinosaur skeleton hanging in the atrium. In the chaos of battle, the humans escape.

The tension of Jurassic Park's final conflict is palpable, and the audience's relief at the escape is an almost audible sigh. As muscles relax and pulse rates subside, it is almost impossible to believe that the experience was a total illusion.

The future has just begun. As startling and realistic as the digital dinosaurs were in *Jurassic Park*, they are only a hint of what is yet to come from the world of computer graphics.

The Man Behind the Curtain

Unfortunately, since both advertisers and filmmakers understandably prefer to present their visions to us as whole and complete, we viewers rarely get to see what goes on behind the scenes. We get the flash and the wow, but we're left wondering how it was ever possible to achieve the effect we just experienced without serious injury to the actors involved or incalculable cost to the sponsor.

Courtesy of Carolco. © 1991

As cool as ice, the silvery T1000 walks out of the flames of his fiery crash in *Terminator 2*.

It is precisely this behind-the-scenes view that we hope to convey in the following sections of this book. We will first look at how computer graphics all began, explore the hardware devices and software techniques that make computer imagery possible, examine the various computer-based techniques used to create visual effects; and finally, take a detailed look at how those techniques have been used in specific films, television commercials, and long-format animations.

© 1993, Tyco Industries.

Dr. Zub looks at Ted, one of his star crash dummies, snoring away after a hard test that has left him in pieces.

The truth of the matter is, however, that not only was it an illusion to the audience, but also to each of the film's actors. In this dramatic final encounter, they saw neither living dinosaurs nor even a model of the carnivorous killers. These dinosaurs were entirely created and animated on a computer, and later composited into the final film print, long after the actors had been shot reacting to their imaginary attackers.

Visual Illusion Runs Deep

Yet, the illusion of film and video runs even deeper, involving all aspects of the film and video production process. At its most basic level, a moving picture is not really moving at all. It is, in fact, a series of still photographs run quickly past a light source or shot from the back of a cathode ray tube (the picture tubes used for televisions and computer monitors). In the case of feature films, the still pictures change at the rate of 24 frames per second. Video, due to the cycle time of U.S. electrical current, increases this rate to 30 frames a second.

These speeds are too fast for our brains to notice the gaps between the frames, and so our minds are fooled into creating a smooth and seamless progression of action. And this is only the beginning of the illusion, because film and video special effects is more than just the capturing and playing back of recorded actions: it is a complex, multi-layered process by which each frame is built up from many separate, often disconnected, elements (such as blue-screen photography, computer-controlled cameras and models, matte paintings, live action, puppetry, and computer imagery).

Computer-generated flying vehicles of all sorts glide peacefully through a future utopia at the Luxor Hotel in Las Vegas.

Beyond Science Fiction

Since the late 1970s, the computer, with its rapidly expanding capability to create illusion and control visual reality, has made its way to the heart of virtually all of these processes. Thanks to the computer, directors are now finding themselves suddenly freed from the constraints of time and space. They are discovering that not only can the computer be used to realize their visions of science fiction-based realities, such as in *The Abyss* or *Terminator 2*, but also to successfully plan and produce more real-world dramas and comedies, such as *Line of Fire*, *Toys*, and *Striking Distance*.

While film production may account for the most glamorous and highest-visibility uses of computer graphics, commercial television is where the computer found its first home in the entertainment industry and still finds its widest use. With its more generous per-minute advertising budgets and more limited technical requirements, television advertising has been the primary developer and consumer of computer graphics imagery since the science of making pictures with computers began over two decades ago. It is here that many of the most startling techniques, which have animated everything from twisting Toyotas to Scrubbing Bubbles, were first developed and presented to the public.

How It All Began

In the beginning, computer graphics were as cumbersome and as hard to control as dinosaurs must have been in their own time. Like dinosaurs, the hardware systems, or muscles, of early computer graphics were huge and ungainly. The machines often filled entire buildings. Also like dinosaurs, the software programs or brains of computer graphics were hopelessly underdeveloped. Fortunately for the visual arts, the evolution of both the brains and brawn of computer graphics did not require a hundred million years to develop. It has, instead, taken a mere three decades to move the science and art of making pictures with computers out of the stone age and into the leading edge of the silicon era.

Glass couples dance in stereographic imagery at one of the three film-based attractions created for the Luxor Las Vegas Hotel by the Trumbull Company.

©1974, Edwin Catmull.

Created at the University of Utah, this mathematical shape, called a Kline Bottle, was one of the first fully shaded curved surfaces.

Drawing the First Line

Imagine sitting at a computer without any visual feedback on a monitor. There would be no spreadsheets, no word processors, not even a simple game of solitaire. This is what it was like in the early days of computers. The only way to interact with a computer at that time was through toggle switches, flashing lights, and Teletype printouts.

In 1962, all this began to change. In that year, Ivan Sutherland, then a Ph.D. student at the Massachusetts Institute of Technology (MIT), created the science of computer graphics. For his dissertation, he wrote a program called Sketchpad that allowed him to draw lines of light directly on a cathode ray tube (CRT). The results were simple and primitive—a cube, a series of lines, groups of simple geometric figures—but they offered an entirely new vision of how computers could be used.

Starting an Industry

In 1964, Sutherland teamed up with Dr. David Evans at the University of Utah to develop the world's first academic computer graphics department. Their goal was to attract only the most gifted students from across the country by creating a unique department that combined hard science with the creative arts. They knew they were starting a brand new industry and wanted people who would be able to lead that industry out of its infancy.

Out of their unique mix of science and art, a basic understanding of computer graphics began to grow. Algorithms, for the creation of solid objects, their modeling, lighting, and shading, poured forth. The roots of virtually every aspect of today's computer graphics industry, from desktop publishing to virtual reality, find their beginnings in the basic research that came out of the University of Utah in the 60s and early 70s.

> Algorithms are the series of steps a computer must take to achieve a certain result.

The First Computer Graphics Company

During this time, Evans and Sutherland also founded the first computer graphics company. Aptly named Evans & Sutherland (E&S), the company was established in 1968 and rolled out its first computer graphics systems in 1969.

Up until that time, the only computers available that could create pictures were custom-designed for the military and prohibitively expensive. E&S's computer system could draw wireframe images extremely rapidly, and was the first commercial "workstation" created for computer-aided design (CAD). It found its earliest customers in both the automotive and aerospace industries.

What's a Wireframe?

Computer images can be created in two different ways: either as a series of lines or as a series of shaded surfaces. Line-based drawings are called wireframe images because the object shown is made up of a series of separate lines. It's as if a collection of thin wires were bent in the shape of the object. Where there are no wires, the viewer can see through to the other side.

For solid-looking computer images, the spaces between the wires must be filled in, either with colors or shades of gray. This requires the use of what is called a frame buffer, which is described in detail in the upcoming hardware chapter.

Beyond Utah

Throughout its early years, the University of Utah's Computer Science Department was generously supported by a series of research grants from the Department of Defense. The 1970s, with its anti-war and anti-military protests, brought increasing restriction to the flow of aca-

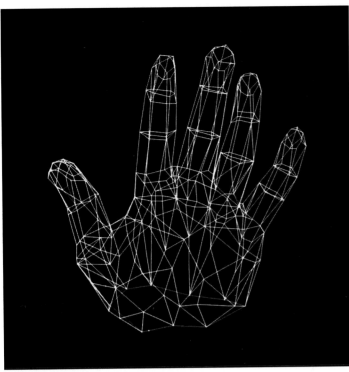

Edwin Catmull's hand in wireframe. Each point was painstakingly digitized using a mechanical 3-D digitizer.

Other Efforts Begin

Other academic computer graphics programs appeared at Ohio State University in 1965 under the direction of artist Charles Csuri, at Cornell University's School of Architecture in 1967, headed by Donald Greenberg, and at the University of Illinois at Chicago in 1973, led by Thomas DeFanti.

The Schure Thing

To this end, Schure hired Edwin Catmull, a University of Utah Ph.D., to head the NYIT computer graphics lab and then equipped the lab with the best graphics hardware available. When completed, the lab boasted over $2 million of equipment.

The staff, many of whom also came from the University of Utah, was given free reign to develop both two- and three-dimensional computer graphics tools, with the goal of soon producing a full-length, computer-animated feature film. The effort, which began in 1973, produced dozens of research papers and hundreds of new discoveries, but in the end, it was far too early for such a complex undertaking. The computers of that time were simply too expensive and too underpowered, and the software not nearly developed enough.

By 1978, Schure could no longer justify funding such an expensive effort, and the lab's funding was cut back. The

demic grants, which had a direct impact on the Utah department's ability to carry out research. Fortunately, as the program wound down, Dr. Alexander Schure, founder and president of New York Institute of Technology (NYIT), stepped forward with his dream of creating computer-animated feature films.

Today, complex models, such as this termite with over 60,000 points, can easily be created.

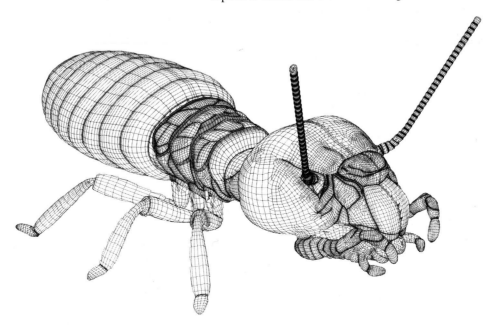

Cylinders, spheres, and a digitized keyboard make up this early computer graphic image of skeleton hands working a computer keyboard.

ironic thing is that had the Institute decided to patent many more of its researcher's seminal discoveries than it did, it would control much of the technology in use today. Fortunately for the industry as a whole, however, this did not happen. Instead, the research was made available to whomever could make good use of it, thus accelerating the technology's development.

Courtesy of Alvy Ray Smith.

Moving the Computer into Film and Television

As NYIT's influence started to wane, the first wave of commercial computer graphics studios began to appear. Film visionary George Lucas (creator of the immensely successful *Star Wars* and *Indiana Jones* trilogies) hired Catmull from NYIT in 1978 to start the Lucasfilm Computer Development Division, and a group of over a half-dozen computer graphics studios around the country opened for business. While Lucas's computer division began researching how to apply digital technology to

filmmaking, the other studios began creating flying logos and broadcast graphics for various corporations including TRW, Gillette, the National Football League, and television programs, such as "The NBC Nightly News" and "ABC World News Tonight."

Although it was the dream of these initial computer graphics companies to make movies with their computers, virtually all the early commercial computer graphics were created for television. It was and still is easier and far more profitable to create graphics for television commercials than for film. A typical frame of film requires many more computer calculations than a similar image created for

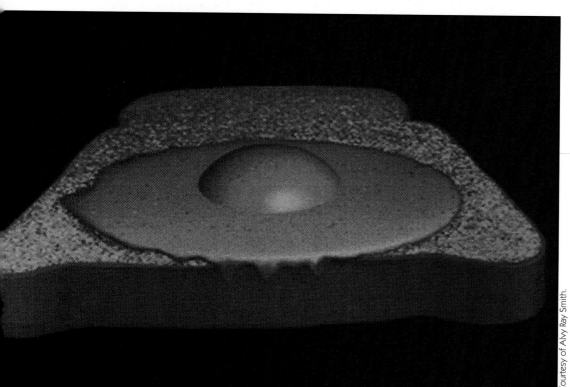

To create this early computer graphics image, computer scientist Alvy Ray Smith took a spaceship someone else had developed, changed its colors, and laid it on top of a 3-D toast model he had developed. He then used an early digital paint system to paint the surfaces of the objects and produced one of the first images to combine both 2- and 3-dimensional computer imagery.

Courtesy of Alvy Ray Smith.

Known for their high-quality broadcast graphics, Pacific Data Images (PDI) produced this opening for the NBC Monday Night at the Movies.

Following their earliest television graphics with Globo TV of Brazil, PDI worked on a number of show openings for ABC, including this piece for ABC Wide World of Sports.

ABC Sports, Inc.©1985.

television, while per-second film budgets provide only about one-third as much income.

The Forgettable Debut

The almost insurmountable technical and monetary obstacles posed by film help to explain why the feature film debut of computer graphics was such a singularly forgettable event. The grand debut came in the 1976 film, *Future World*, and consisted of a few brief seconds of actor Peter Fonda's computer-generated head and a computer-generated hand modeled by Edwin Catmull while he was a student at the University of Utah, shown on computer monitors in the background. It was clearly not something to galvanize the entertainment industry into action, but even so, it did serve notice that a brand new way of making film images was on the horizon.

Wake-Up Call

The actual wake-up call to the entertainment industry was not to come until five years later with the 1982 release of

Star Trek II: The Wrath of Kahn. That movie contained a prodigious sixty seconds of the most exciting full-color computer graphics yet seen. Called the "Genesis Effect," the sequence starts out with a view of a dead planet, as barren as an asteroid, hanging lifeless in space. A crescent of the sun is just beginning to show along the right limn of the planet. The camera spirals slowly in towards the rock from thousands of miles out, following a missile's trail. The missile, tipped with a life-creating warhead called Genesis, impacts on the planet. Flames arc outward and race across the surface, as the camera zooms in tight. Running before the fires, it records the planet's

The Genesis Effect has been completed and the planet has been brought to life. The camera swings in across the ocean below and smashes into the mountains on the other side. Fortunately, the mountain was only digital and could be told to move.

Watch Out for That Mountain!

There was, however, one error in the *Star Trek* sequence that did not show up until all the frames had been completely computed. The camera move that swept the point of view across the developing landscape as mountains shot up around it, inadvertently dragged the camera directly through the face of one of the mountains. Because of the unpredictable nature of fractal mountain generation, it was impossible to see this ahead of time. To change the camera move to fit the mountain would have required recomputing more frames than they had time for. So instead, they simply cut a digital canyon through the side of the mountain to let the camera pass untouched.

transformation from molten whites and reds to cool blues and greens as mountains thrust upward and oceans fill with water. The final scene spirals the camera back out into space, revealing the cloud-swirled, newly born planet.

While these sixty seconds may seem a small accomplishment in light of current digital effects, this remarkable scene, created by Lucasfilm's Computer Division, represented many firsts. It required the development of several radically new computer graphics algorithms, including one for creating convincing computer fire and another to produce realistic mountains and shorelines from fractal equations. Fractal equations are often simple-looking mathematical formulas that can create infinitely complex images in computer graphics.

In addition, this sequence was the first time computer graphics was used as the center of attention, instead of being used merely as a prop to support other action. No one in the entertainment industry had seen anything like it, and it unleashed a flood of queries from Hollywood directors seeking to find out both how it was done and whether an entire film could be created in this fashion. Unfortunately, with the release of *TRON* later that same year and *The Last Starfighter* in 1984, the answer was still a decided no.

The wake-up begins. The Genesis rocket has struck the dead planet, bringing it and computer graphics to life.

Right Effects, Wrong Movie

TRON, released in the fall of 1982, was to be Disney's triumphant return to feature film production. In its promotional campaign, it was touted as a technological tour de force, which, in fact, it was. The film contained over 15 minutes of fully computer-animated shots plus another twenty-five minutes in which computer animation was composited with live action. The quantity of computer imagery dwarfed (by many times) the sum of all computer graphic imagery developed for film up to that time. Its production required the collaboration of four of the top computer graphics studios of the times, MAGI, Triple-I, Robert Abel & Associates, and Digital Effects.

The film's graphics were extremely well executed, the best seen up to that point, but they could not save the film from its weak script. Unfortunately, the technology was greatly oversold during the film's promotion and so in the end it was the technology that took the blame for the film's failure.

Starting with a Bang

This period of the early 80s saw further expansion in the ranks of existing computer graphics studios. Two in particular, Digital Productions in Los Angeles and Pacific Data Images (PDI) near San Francisco represented the opposite ends of the spectrum of how the industry was to evolve. Digital Productions was started in 1982 by programmer Gary Demos and producer John Whitney, Jr., who spun off from Triple-I. They understood that creating film-quality computer graphic imagery required the maximum amount of processing power available. Everyone in the industry knew what it took and had invested heavily in very expensive high-speed computers. In starting Digital productions, however, Demos and

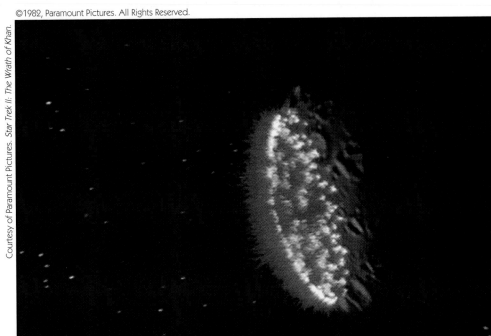

The Genesis fires spread, racing across the planet in 60 seconds that shook Hollywood and promised a new future in filmmaking.

Digital Productions would suck up all the available commercial computer graphics work, leaving nothing for anyone else. As if to confirm this suspicion, Lorimar Productions immediately hired them to begin work on the special effects for the *Last Starfighter*, a science fiction film due for release in 1984. Using their Cray, Digital Productions created over twenty minutes of the most detailed and complex computer-generated space-based scenes yet shown. Additionally, an amazing ten minutes of computer-generated effects were cut from the film in the final editing process. This was the first time that expensive digital imagery had wound up on the cutting room floor. Regrettably, this film also suffered from a weak story line. While it was not the financial failure that *TRON* was, it once again did not live up to the promotional overselling of the technology, and so computer graphics suffered.

Meanwhile, behind the scenes, computer graphics were beginning to get real. Created by Robert Cook and others at Pixar, this image showed gorgeous reflections, motion blur, and penumbras never before seen together in one image.

Whitney appeared to trump them all with the unheard of purchase of a $10.5 million Cray X-MP supercomputer.

When Digital Productions announced their purchase, the rest of the industry went into shock. Everyone thought that with this much processing power at their command,

Starting with a Peep

PDI, on the other hand, began much more modestly. In 1980, it consisted only of founder Carl Rosendahl, just out of Stanford, and a Cromemco personal computer. In his first year of business, production income reached the astounding level of $500. Rosendahl was not particularly concerned, however, because the lack of work gave him time to research his chosen profession. It was also during

The holographic display of the planet Endor in George Lucas' Return of the Jedi was created in 3-D graphics.

this time that he met his future partners, Richard Chuang and Glenn Entis, and pitched in with them to buy a PDP 11-44 computer from Digital Equipment Corporation.

They used this primitive PDP to create their first portfolio of flying logo animations, showing full antialiasing and 24-bit color for the 1982 SIGGRAPH computer graphics conference. This first reel landed them a lucrative contract for Globo TV of Brazil, which hired them to create four spots consisting of flying logos and show openings. The results astounded everyone and left PDI with cash in the bank, a brand new Vax 11/750 computer, and a new name in the industry: Three boys and a VAX.

The boys subsequently went on to build a reputation for creating some of the best broadcast graphics in the industry, animated openings for "Entertainment Tonight" in 1983 and the Winter Olympics in 1984, followed by four years of ABC Sports. Throughout this time, they continued to build their business entirely from their own cash flow. Instead of searching for major investors to provide the cash to buy the expensive computers used by the other larger studios, they concentrated on networking what they could afford. This strategy, whether through blind luck or deliberate design, was to save them from extinction as the workstation revolution hit the computer graphics world in the mid '80s.

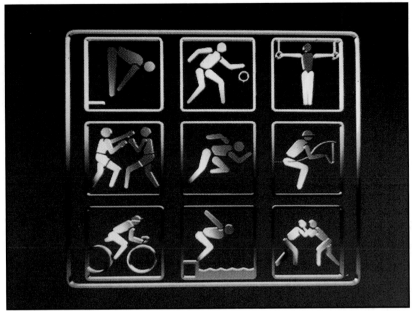

PDI animated openings for ABC's broadcast of the 1984 Olympics.

Good-Bye Old Guard

With the 1980s came the age of personal computers and dedicated workstations (powerful minicomputers that were cheap enough to buy for one person). Smaller was better, faster, and much, much cheaper. Advances in silicon chip technologies brought massive and very rapid increases in power to smaller computers along with drastic reductions in prices. The costs of commercial graphics plunged to match, to the point where the major studios suddenly could no longer cover the mountains of debt coming due on their overpriced, centralized hardware.

With their expenses mounting and without the extra capital to upgrade to the newer cheaper com-

PDI's 1986 short film, Chromosaurus, was an early attempt to create living computer-generated creatures.

The new Death Star orbits Endor covered in a protective energy shield. Graphics were filmed off a high-resolution screen in black and white. Color was added optically as the image elements were layered together to create the final frames.

puters, virtually every independent computer graphics studio went out of business by 1987. All of them, that is, except PDI, which went on to become the largest commercial computer graphics house in the business and to serve as the model for the next wave of studios.

Digital Dearth

As the commercial computer graphics industry fell apart, computer effects for feature films came to a grinding halt. The only group left with the capability of creating such imagery was the division begun at Lucasfilm in 1978, and unfortunately for them, George Lucas seemed intent on using this division for other things. From its inception, this group had been pursuing the goal of applying digital technology to various aspects of the filmmaking process. The area they chose to attack first was that of digital film compositing, and to that end they built the world's first digital laser film scanner. Though difficult to maintain and somewhat finicky when in use, this was truly a remarkable device for its time, capable of scanning at resolutions up to 4,000 pixels per line across a single frame of film.

While Lucas did in fact use his Computer Division for two short computer-animated film sequences, the first for *The Return of the Jedi* in 1983, and the second for *The Young Sherlock Holmes* in 1985, it had become obvious that Lucas' film company and its computer graphics wing were going in very

different directions. As a result, the decision was made in 1985 to spin the division out on its own under the name of Pixar. By 1986, the transition was completed as Lucas sold his controlling interest to Steve Jobs, the founder of Apple Computers.

Film Graphics Rebuilds

Burned twice by *TRON* and *The Last Starfighter*, and frightened by the financial failure of virtually the entire industry, Hollywood steered clear of computer graphics for several years. Behind the scenes, however, it was building back and waiting for that next big break.

The break materialized in the form of a watery creation for James Cameron's 1989 film, *The Abyss*. For this film, the group at George Lucas' Industrial Light & Magic (ILM) created the first completely computer-generated, entirely organic looking and thoroughly believable creature to be realistically integrated with live action footage and characters. This was the watery pseudopod that snaked its way into the underwater research lab to get

Glass couples dance in stereographic imagery at one of the three film-based attractions created for the Luxor Las Vegas Hotel by the Trumbull Company.

Never before had live action and computer graphics interacted in this way. Industrial Light & Magic's execution of James Cameron's water creature for the 1989 film, *The Abyss*, promised a whole new future in filmmaking.

a closer look at its human inhabitants. In this stunning effect, ILM overcame two very difficult problems: producing a soft-edged, bulgy, and irregularly shaped object, and convincingly anchoring that object in a live-action sequence.

Just as the 1982 Genesis sequence served as the wake-up call for early film computer graphics, this sequence for *The Abyss* was the announcement that computer graphics had finally come of age. A massive outpouring of computer-generated film graphics has since ensued with studios from across the gamut participating in the action. From that point on, digital technology spread so rapidly that the movies using digital effects have become too numerous to list in entirety. However, they include the likes of *Total Recall, Toys, Terminator 2: Judgment Day, The Babe, In the Line of Fire, Death Becomes Her,* and, of course, *Jurassic Park.*

Bursting at the Seams

Much has happened in the commercial computer graphics industry since the decline of the first wave of studios and the rise of the second. Software and hardware costs have plummeted. The number of well-trained animators and programmers has increased dramatically. And at last, Hollywood and the advertising community have acknowledged that the digital age has arrived, this time not to disappear. All these factors have lead to an explosion in both the size of existing studios and the number of new enterprises opening their doors.

As the digital tide continues to rise, only one thing is certain. We have just begun to see how computer technology will change the visual arts.

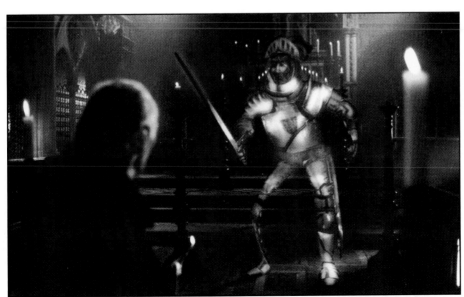

The stained-glass man from Lucasfilm's 1986 movie, *The Young Sherlock Holmes,* was the first animated living creature anyone ever attempted to create for a feature film.

Hardware: The Brains and Brawn

Hardware is the physical stuff of computer graphics—its eyes, hands, brain circuitry, and brawn. Its rapid and continued development is what has made commercial computer graphics a viable industry. Because of the increasing power and decreasing prices of modern processors (the brains of the computer) and peripherals (scanners, printers, monitors, and so on), 3-dimensional computer imagery is finding its way into everything from home computer games to television shows, commercials, and feature films.

This growing ease of access to the 3-D digital world, however, is only a very recent phenomenon. Throughout most of its development, computer graphics has been plagued with hardware limitations, such as low-resolution monitors, underpowered processing units, and a lack of suitable means of output, all of which have conspired to prevent visual artists from making full use of the medium.

On the hardware level, the process of creating computer graphics imagery involves three primary steps: getting 3-D image information into the digital world and displaying it, manipulating it once it is there, and then pulling it back out once it is complete. Looking at the hardware involved in each of these steps will help explain the complexities of the art and science of making pictures with computers.

A utopian vision of the future from "The Theatre of Time." Without today's most advanced computers, Douglas Trumbull's vision of the future for the Luxor Las Vegas Hotel would not have been possible.

Monitor Displays: Hello in There . . .

While in the past, engineers toggled programs into the computer with manual switches and then watched light displays for the results, the primary contact with a computer today is through the monitor. It has become our window into the digital world and through that world into deeper levels of our own reality. Doctors use it to peer inside the human body without surgery. Scientists studying everything from genetic engineering to galactic evolution, gaze through this window to catch glimpses of what is not visible with any other scientific tool. And artists use it to view and capture their own visions of reality.

Graphics on computer have become second nature to us all. Typing commands by hand, instead of pointing at an image and clicking a mouse, is becoming increasingly rare. Not a single computer system is sold in this country, and perhaps the world, that does not use ever more sophisticated graphical interfaces. Yet, how is it that we see what

we see? What makes this window into other worlds work so well?

Computer Monitors: On the Beam

Essentially, computer monitors are just like television tubes. They are made up of a sealed vacuum tube, an electron gun, and a screen of colored phosphors. The gun, mounted at the back of the tube, fires a beam of electrons, which is swept rapidly back and forth across the screen. As the beam hits the screen, a picture is built up line by line from top to bottom. The scanning process happens so fast that our eye can't see the individual lines, and our brain interprets the entire screen as a single image. Whether the image is moving or still, the monitor redraws the entire screen 30 times a second.

Frame Buffers: Hold It Right There!

While the new interactive television boom is beginning to change television technology, standard television does not offer precise control of each part of the displayed image. It is not necessary because the presented imagery is intended

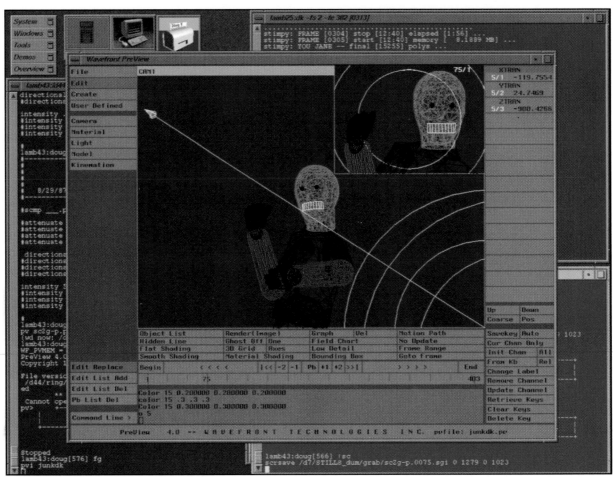

A typical high-end monitor screen. Here it shows two wireframe views of one of the Crash Dummies as it is being animated.

for passive viewing only. Computer monitors, on the other hand, demand this control. Without access to each picture element, called a pixel, everything from word processing to computer animation would be impossible.

> Resolution refers to the density of pixels on a computer monitor and in a computer image. The greater the number of pixels in an image, the higher the resolution.

In the digital world, the CRT screen is chopped up into a grid of these pixels. (The number of pixels on a standard monitor screen is 640 pixels wide by 480 high.) The contents of each of these pixels is represented by a digital number held in an area of the computer memory called the frame buffer. The size of the frame buffer is directly

Input Devices: Turning the Outside In

Mousing About

Now that the window into the digital world is in place, how does something conceived outside in the real world get transported to the other side of the glass? There are several approaches that use different tools of varying complexity. The first is with the simple and ubiquitous devices of the mouse, stylus, and keyboard. This is the primary approach used by virtually every computer graphics studio operating today, whether they are working in film or television.

Using software designed for 3-D modeling, a modeler sits at the computer and draws lines on the computer monitor screen using either a stylus and drawing pad, or a

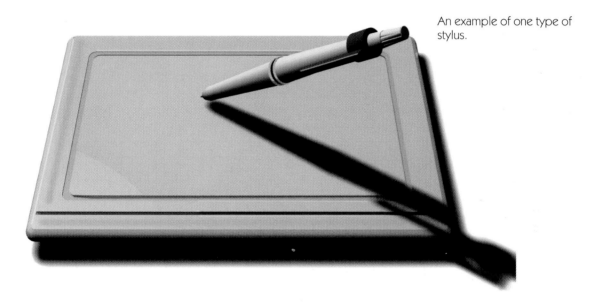

An example of one type of stylus.

related to the monitor's resolution, plus the number of colors that can be displayed simultaneously.

Generally, the high-end computer graphics created for film and television require the best of monitors. These often have resolutions of up to 2,000 x 1,250 pixels and can display millions of colors at the same time. Of course, these are also the most expensive monitors, both in terms of dollars as well as amount of data that must be moved around inside the computer to create a picture. In the past, when computer memory was extremely expensive, the size of the frame buffer represented a real limit to what could be displayed and manipulated interactively. Today, since many high-end graphics machines can be configured with hundreds of megabytes (millions of bytes) of memory, this limitation is all but disappearing.

mouse. The monitor displays what has just been drawn, and the data representing the associated geometric information of the object being built are stored in a file on disk. Gradually, line-by-line, the structure is created until the desired form is reached. The process is somewhat akin to building a physical model in the real world, and it can take anywhere from a few hours to many months, depending on the structure's complexity.

Through the Looking Glass

There are situations, however, where it is more economical to start with an existing physical object. This is very useful for complex shapes like the human body, or for props whose computer representation must be identical to the actual objects used in a live-action scene. The process of converting a physical object into a computer model is called digitizing or scanning. Currently, there are two primary methods of scanning in use today, one that uses magnetic fields and one that employs laser technology.

Magnets

For magnetic scanners, the object to be digitized is first covered with a grid of fine lines, which are packed closely together in areas that need greater detail and farther apart in areas that don't. The grid is a necessary guide for the modeler and helps create a regular, evenly spaced collection of surface areas.

The object is then placed inside a strong magnetic field, and an electronic pointer is then touched to each of the mesh intersections covering the object. The process is painstaking and can often require digitizing thousands of points for a single object. Its primary benefit for commercial applications is that complex shapes, which are extremely difficult to create in any other way, can still be used for computer graphics effects.

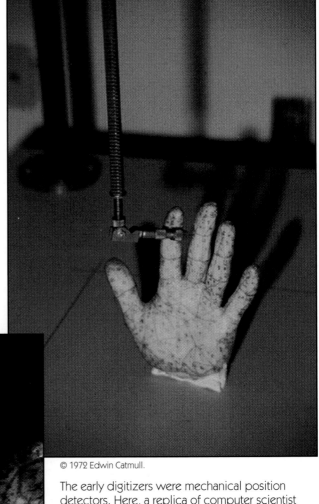

The early digitizers were mechanical position detectors. Here, a replica of computer scientist Edwin Catmull's hand is digitized point by point.

And Lasers

Optical systems using lasers offer an entirely different approach that is much quicker, yet has certain drawbacks. 3-D laser scanners require no gridding and thus do away with the laborious task of touching each grid point manually. The object to be digitized is placed inside the scanning area, and a laser beam is shined on it. The dimensions of the resulting computer model are calculated based on the reflection of the laser pulses from the various surfaces. The process is fast, taking only a few minutes per object, thus opening the possibility of scanning live models.

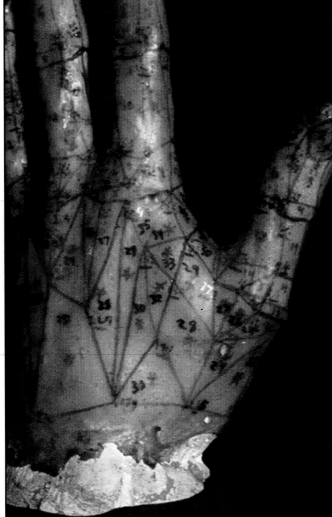

A close-up of the hand in the previous picture shows the grid pattern that was followed to digitize the hand. See Chapter 1 to see the resulting wireframe structure.

Sculptor Diana Walczak, co-founder of the Hollywood computer graphics company, Kleiser-Walczak Construction Co., digitizes one of her creations. Each intersection of the grid shown on the model must be touched with the magnetic digitizing wand in her hand.

There are several difficulties, however, that tend to limit its use. The size of a laser-scannable object is much smaller than for the magnetic approach because of the need to move a physical laser around it. Objects with complex surfaces are difficult to scan correctly because protrusions of surface elements can block the laser light from reaching hidden parts. And laser scanners offer little control over the amount of detail gathered. Some areas of a model, particularly those areas that flex or bend, are more important than others, requiring a finer level of scanned information. Unfortunately, the laser scans everything equally. Despite these limitations, however, they have found widespread use in areas where speed is of the essence.

But Everything Is Not 3-D

While the above methods provide ways to enter 3-dimensional data directly into the computer, it does not address how to work with 2-dimensional images such as film. Since film is the medium for all motion pictures and is also the medium used to record live-action imagery for most television commercials, it is of paramount importance to be able to work with it. The primary difficulty with film, as opposed to video, in the digital world is that its resolution requirements are extremely high. Both the color range and the image density is much greater for film.

The scanners developed by Kodak for its Cinecite Installations and by Industrial Light & Magic (ILM) for its special effects work create a 38-megabyte file for each film frame. An entire 200-megabyte personal computer disk would be filled to capacity after only five frames of film. When you consider that a feature film is generally over 125,000 frames, the quantities of data to move and manipulate become astronomical. It is only recently with advances in storage and processor technologies that digital film manipulation has actually become possible.

Processing: The Heavy Lifting

Over the few decades that computer hardware has been in existence, computers have gone from sacred objects served by the high priests of technology, to everyday commodities purchased in discount stores or through mail-order catalogs. The price per unit of computing power has dropped to the point where most desktop computers sold today are more powerful than the mainframes of just a few years ago.

Cyberware's (Monterey, CA) laser scanning system. The scanner is mounted on the cabinet in back, while the results of a scan, that of a woman's head, are visible on the monitor in the table in front.

As is evident from the earlier discussions, image computing requires moving and manipulating very large amounts of data very quickly. This is particularly true when trying to animate interactively. Bus speed, processor power, and disk access time must all be extremely fast. Bus speed is the rate at which the computer transfers data to and from its main components. Processor power refers to the number of calculations the computer can complete in a second. And disk access time is the time it takes to retrieve blocks of data from a computer hard disk.

Output: Turning the Inside Out

At last, the effect is created and rendered, and everybody is happy. Or are they? Suddenly the realization hits that this complex reality created inside the computer must now somehow be taken out of the digital world. Fortunately for television, this has never been a serious problem. Since the images are going to be shown on the same monitor-type device as they were created on, the transfer is relatively easy. All that is required is to change the format of

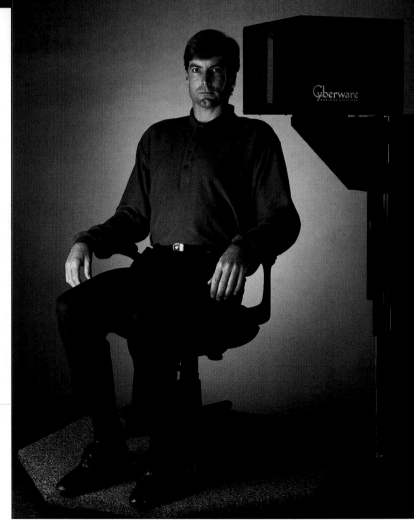

Painless and fast, the laser scanner's red beam plays across the subject's face collecting information about its shape and building a computer model to match.

Like most computer graphics effects houses, ILM's computer lab is loaded with dozens of Silicon Graphics computers.

the electrical signal from digital to what is called analog form and record it on videotape.

Creating Film Frames

Unfortunately for film work, the story is decidedly different. Since motion pictures are recorded on film and projected from film, the ultimate destination of computer graphics imagery for this medium must be a piece of film negative. Given the demands for high-quality, high-resolution images, the process of getting computer images onto film has not been easy.

Currently, there are two primary approaches to the problem. The first is to use lasers to imprint pixels on film, and the second is to use a CRT-based film recorder. The CRT systems have been around the longest and consist of a very high-resolution monitor that is set inside a light-proof box. A camera is trained on this monitor with its shutter open, and the image is recorded through red, green, and blue filters.

As these technologies continue to evolve, the potential is that they will do for

film what digital videotape has done for television. In the future, it is possible that the only time actual film footage will be used in the process of creating a motion picture will be when it is shot in live action and when it is finally output by laser printer for optical copying and release. All of the other steps of compositing, color correction, editing, and so on will take place on computer.

Digital signals are made up of on-and-off pulses of electricity. These pulses represent the ones and zeros that are stored in the computer. Analog signals, on the other hand, are continuous waves that vary gradually in intensity. This form is used for television signals.

With the accelerating developments in computer hardware, from input to output, it is not hard to see that soon hardware will cease to be one of the primary limits in the creation and application of computer graphic imagery.

Lincoln Hu, Senior Technical Director of George Lucas' Industrial Light & Magic (ILM), adjusts ILM's digital film scanner. The film is loaded in the circular magazine on top and passed frame by frame in front of a powerful light source. The frame's image falls on a series of electronic scanners which convert it into digital form.

The Process: Building Worlds and Bringing Them to Life

Creating computer graphics is essentially about three things: modeling, animation, and rendering. Modeling is the process by which 3-dimensional objects are built inside the computer; animation is about making those objects come to life, and rendering is about giving them their ultimate appearance.

Hardware is the brains and brawn of computer graphics, but it is powerless without the right software. It is the software that allows the modeler to build a computer graphic object, that helps an animator bring this object to life, and that, in the end, gives the image its final look. Sophisticated computer graphics software for commercial studios is either purchased for $30,000 to $50,000, or developed in-house. Most studios use a combination of both.

® Used with permission from Pillsbury. Image courtesy of Pacific Data Images.

A low-resolution image was first used to flesh out the animation of the Pillsbury Doughboy before this final, high-resolution image was rendered.

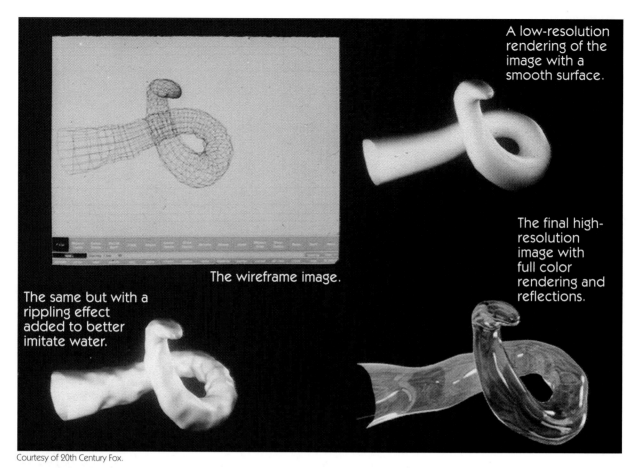

A low-resolution rendering of the image with a smooth surface.

The wireframe image.

The final high-resolution image with full color rendering and reflections.

The same but with a rippling effect added to better imitate water.

Courtesy of 20th Century Fox.

The water creature from James Cameron's 1989 film, *The Abyss*, in various stages of completion.

World Building: More Than Just Pretty Pictures

Modeling in computer graphics is a little like sculpting, a little like building models with wood and glue, and a lot like nothing else in the world. Its flexibility and potential are unmatched in any other art form. With computer graphics it is possible to build entire worlds and entire realities, each with its own laws, its own look, and its own scales of time and space.

Access to these 3-dimensional computer realities, however, is almost always through the 2-dimensional window of the computer monitor. This can lead to the misunderstanding that 3-D modeling is merely the production of carefully executed perspective drawings. This couldn't be farther from the truth. All elements created during any modeling session possess three full dimensions and at any time may be rotated, turned upside down, and viewed from any desired angle or perspective. In addition, they may be rescaled, reshaped, or resized whenever the modeler chooses.

Modeling: The First Step

Modeling is the first step in creating a 3-dimensional computer animation. It requires the artist's ability to visualize mentally the

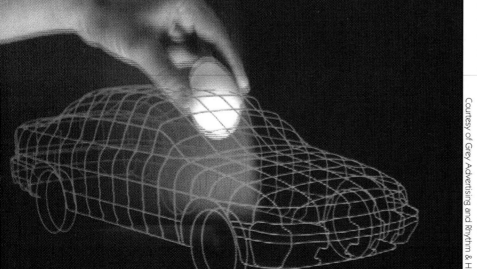

Courtesy of Grey Advertising and Rhythm & Hues.

Here, an initial wireframe image of a Mitsubishi car was used as an element in the final commercial spot.

objects being built, and the craftsperson's painstaking attention to detail to bring it to completion. To create an object, an animator starts with a blank screen and sets the scale of the computer's coordinate system for that element. The scale can be anything from microns to light-years across, and every element can have its own scale. The computer keeps this information associated with the object, wherever it goes, and increases or decreases its apparent size depending upon the scale of the environment into which it is placed. It is important, if two or more objects are going to share the same 3-D space, that they use the same scale. A chair built in inches will disappear in a living room built in yards.

Different Modeling Approaches

Depending upon the complexity of the computer graphic element being modeled, the developer can use any of several approaches. The traditional method is to draw lines on the computer screen with a mouse or stylus, and gradually build up a 3-dimensional structure. Where the structure is too complex to define precisely, surface elements called *patches* can be used to create the appearance of structure. As lines and patches are added, they can be grouped together in single units and manipulated as a whole. So, an entire object at any stage of construction

can be rotated and viewed from any angle in order to add detail where it is needed. This process ends when the last line is tacked on.

Of Polygons And Patches . . .

In early computer modeling systems, surfaces were built up from collections of what are called polygons. Because these polygons were flat, it required extremely small polygons to make smoothly curved surfaces. Unfortunately, the smaller they got, the harder the computer had to work to create the surface.

Eventually, however, the mathematics of irregular surfaces became better understood, and surface elements, called patches, are now used. Today, patches are of virtually any shape and can be connected together in a smoothly continuous fashion, allowing modelers to create almost any shape they desire.

Three separate views of a few of the highly detailed elements needed to create Red, the unicycle in Pixar's short film, *Red's Dream*.

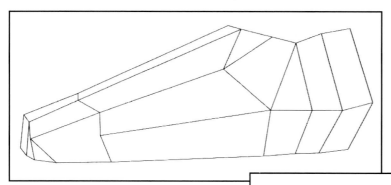

A very low-resolution foot model. For use in areas where no detail is needed.

A medium-resolution foot can have toes and articulated joints, but the surfaces and edges are still somewhat blocky.

© 1993, Viewpoint DataLabs, Orem, Utah 1-800-224-2222.

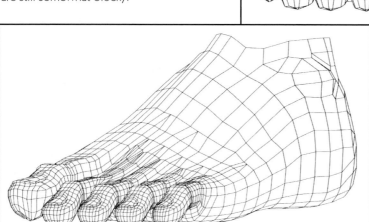

A very detailed foot model that closely resembles a human foot. You can purchase all three of these foot models already built, to avoid putting in the time to create them.

Keeping Libraries in Shape

A second approach is to start the modeling project with one or more geometric shapes chosen from the studio's own graphics library or supplied by the software being used. These shapes are generally the modeling results of their previous work, or selections purchased ready-made from companies, such as Viewpoint DataLabs (Orem, Utah), that sell databases of various shapes ranging from dinosaurs to airplanes.

A wireframe image is made up of a series of thin lines. It does not have solid-looking, shaded surfaces.

Once the starting shape is selected, it is brought up in a wireframe image and presented on the screen. The image appears exactly as it would if the modeler had built it instead of calling it up from a library. It is then possible to add, delete, or change the position of any line or set of points in the image. Once again, the modeler uses a mouse or stylus and selects the areas that need changing. The modeling job is finished when the transformation from original to final new object is complete. This new shape can then be saved to the studio's library for use in future projects.

The important thing to keep in mind when choosing a starting form is that the selected shape should match the desired new object as closely as possible. A close match means fewer changes. When no match is close, it is often faster to create the new model from scratch.

Automatic Model Building: The Digitized Domain

Still another approach to modeling is to use a 3-D digitizer (see "Through the Looking Glass" in Chapter 2 for further details). For complex models, extracting precise dimensions from a real object can be quite time consuming. Every bend and curve must be precisely measured by hand. It is also only the beginning, because those measurements must then be painstakingly used to create that same object line by line on the computer. It's a bit like tearing down a physical model piece by piece, creating a new set of pieces in a different material, and then rebuilding the model with the new pieces. The beauty of the 3-D digitizer is that it eliminates all these steps by recording the dimensions of the object automatically and then building a wireframe model as it goes. The primary drawback to digitizing an object in this way is that it must first be covered with a fine grid of lines to guide the digitizing process.

Laser scanning of real 3-dimensional elements can also be employed to create models automatically. It is much faster than digitizing and so can be used on living objects as well. The difficulty with laser scanners, however, is controlling the amount of data they provide. For example, a laser scanner was used to create an initial computer model of the Tyrannosaurus Rex in *Jurassic Park*. The resulting model was far too detailed to animate easily, and far too complex to simplify. It ended up being used merely as a reference figure to guide the modelers in creating their own computer graphic dinosaur.

A 3-D digitizer is a magnetically based sensing device designed to transform a real 3-dimensional object into a computer graphics model.

Keep the Goal in Mind

With any of these basic approaches, it is important to keep in mind what the object will be used for after it has been completed. If it is simply a set prop like a table or a refrigerator, the modeling will require a small number of lines and patches. If, however, the object must flex or bend, an increasing number of graphic elements must be used in the area that is to be animated. For example, the talking cat created by Rhythm & Hues for the Disney movie *Hocus Pocus*, has a large number of very small patches around the eyes, and a smaller number on the cheeks and head.

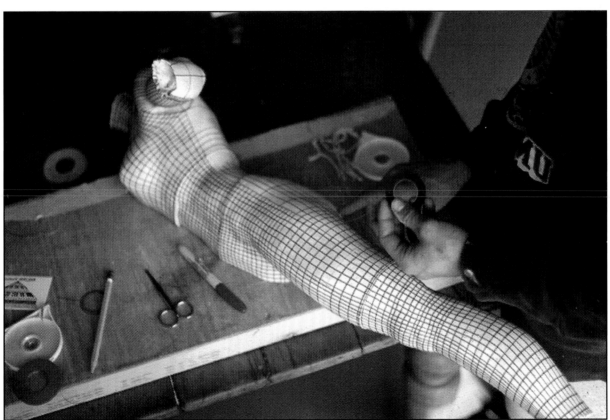

A fine grid is taped onto a sculpture created by Diana Walczak for one of the Luxor Las Vegas Hotel's new film attractions.

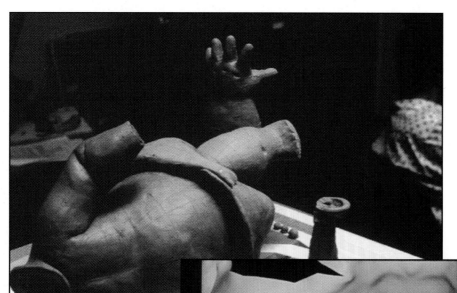

Sculptures of the hand, torso, and leg of the baby in Pixar's Oscar-winning *Tin Toy* prior to laser scanning are shown here.

The resulting computer model of the *Tin Toy* baby's face created by laser scanner.

Each of these patches represents a movable element for animating the face. The more of them there are in any area, the smoother the motion of that area will be. As with everything in computer graphics, this extra flexibility comes at a price. It requires more time for the animator to create the model and more time for the computer to render its final appearance. The density of the patches also has a direct effect on how the surface of an object looks. For any complex surface, the greater the number of patches, the smoother the surface when it is finally rendered.

Once the modeling is complete, it is time to gather the various objects into their appropriate sets and start animating.

Animation: Let There Be Life!

While it is the modeler who possesses the power of creation, it is the animator who provides the spark of life. Reaching across the gulf that separates the real from the digital worlds, the animator breathes life into the collection of computer graphics objects and makes them move.

At its most basic level, the impression of life begins with movement. If something moves on its own in the real world, we tend to think it is alive. The same applies to the animated world, where movement can be communicated through the objects themselves as well as the camera recording the scene. Yet, motion alone is not enough. Flying logos and broadcast graphics move, but no one would say they were alive. Life requires a sense of individual character, of emotion and intent, which arises not only from simple movement, but also from the manner in which the movement is executed.

This sense of character, however, is not something that can be created with any single effect. Rather, it is built up from a collection of techniques, such as staging, anticipation, squash-and-stretch, and exaggeration that have been developed over the 60 years that 2-D cel animation has been in existence. The use of these various rules of animation create the feelings of mass, size, impact, and intent that make an animated world believable and that bring a character to life. For example, it is the exaggerated vibration traveling up Wile E. Coyote's arm and shaking his entire body that shows both the power of his misdirected crowbar swipe at the Roadrunner and the solidity of the rock he hit instead. Similarly, it is the stretching of Daffy Duck's neck as his body runs away from Elmer Fudd that gives him mass and tells us how much he really wants to escape.

While all of these rules for communicating character have become second nature in 2-D animation, when a third dimension is added, it is not immediately apparent how to make them all work. In a perspective environment, where things are not simply in front or in back of

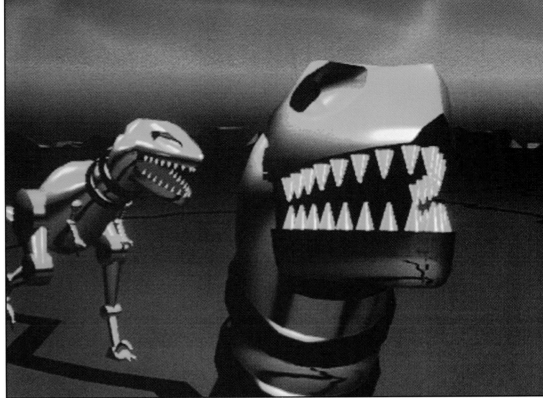

In one of its first in-house film projects, Pacific Data Images (PDI) brought to life a herd of extinct chromosauruses. They had mechanically jointed arms and legs and flexible tails, and ran nimbly across a forbidding barren landscape.

something else as in 2-D animation, how do you make the structure of an element deform smoothly for squash-and-stretch? What aspects of the animated 3-D element can or should be exaggerated? What are the mathematics of such alterations so the computer can create a believable look?

These were not easy artistic or technical questions to answer, but to a large extent they have been answered. Commercial graphics elements like Listerine bottles, Scrubbing Bubbles, and animated automobiles now squash and stretch with growing ease. Short film characters like the Train in PDI's *Locomotion* or the

In a classic cartoon sequence, Andrèo points Wally in one direction and disappears in the other. In a 3-D application of squash-and-stretch, his arm stays in frame as his body makes a getaway.

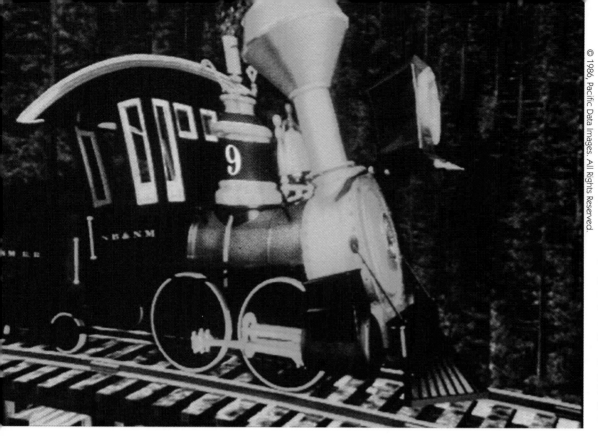

To create a strong sense of the train's reluctance, fear, and eventual determination, in its 1989 short film hit, *Locomotion*, PDI had to develop software to twist and distort the body of a seemingly solid steam locomotive.

Snowman in Pixar's *Knick Knack* use staging, exaggeration, and anticipation as well as any 2-D character ever did.

What's more, new rules are also beginning to evolve. Worlds with apparently different physics are crossing the boundaries between them. Photo-realistic elements, such as the Nissan NX in Rhythm & Hues' "Time Machine" advertisement, or the Unicycle in Pixar's *"Red's Dream,"* deform in quasi-cartoon fashion to communicate emotion, even though they appear to be members of the real world. Real-looking animals, such as the Cat in Disney's film *Hocus Pocus*, are speaking English with believable mouth and lip movements instead of just flapping jaws. Computer animation, however, is an art and science that is still very young, and its potential remains largely unexplored. Perhaps in 60 years, the time it took 2-D cel animation to mature, we might have some inkling of where it can take us.

The Life-Giving Process

Every animation process begins essentially the same way, with a storyboard. A storyboard is a series of hand-drawn sketches, either on paper or on computer, that communicate the story's plot, its action, and the

Film, Video, and Character Animation

By and large, the types of computer animation created for video and for film have been two very different products. As the technology has matured, ever larger amounts of video-based computer animation has become what is called character animation. Dow Bathroom Cleaner's Scrubbing Bubbles come alive and zoom around the bathroom cleaning with wild abandon. "Gilda" the sexy spokes-ant for Volkswagon Polo cars talks seductively with a human interviewer. Generally, the action takes place within the confines of a cartoon world. Or if it is mixed with live action, it is meant to take the viewer toward the cartoon world and away from reality.

Computer animation for film, on the other hand, has largely been used for the opposite purpose. There, computer graphic elements are used to pull the viewer further into the reality of the film. If the T1000 in *Terminator 2* or the dinosaurs in *Jurassic Park* were not something we could see as part of our own world, the believability of the stories would have suffered greatly. In these cases, character is not added through the various comic techniques inherited from Disney cel animation. Instead, it flows from creating a more photo-realistic and behavioral similarity to what we see everyday.

characters involved. The storyboard also defines the look of both the sets and the characters, which in turn determines the character-animation techniques that can be used to carry the story forward.

For example, the "Crash Dummies" characters (the first half-hour cartoon produced entirely in 3-D graphics) had to behave in ways that were similar to the actual toys. The sets and characters had hard, fixed edges, eliminating the technique of squash-and-stretch for communicating both character and mass. On the other hand, the animators at Pixar needed a more cartoon-like feeling for the Listerine bottle in their "Swinging Bottle" commercial, because it did not speak and had virtually no other way of expressing its character.

Courtesy of Sunbeam-Oster and Rhythm & Hues.

In a hilarious commercial created by Rhythm & Hues, the kitchen is turned upside down by the arrival of the new Sunbeam Express Meals appliance. Here, the toaster stretches back in fear before jumping out the open window.

The storyboard also provides the shapes and sizes of the various props, and so this step precedes any 3-D modeling. As the modeling takes place, an animatic of the storyboard is produced. The storyboard is first broken down into scenes, and each scene into shots. The key storyboard stills for each shot are then videotaped and cut together with a test sound track. This, in turn, gives the animation director a good first estimate of the number of frames in each scene.

Who Does What?

Animation assignments are given to individual animators in primarily two ways. For long format pieces with

The Crash Dummies team watches the fireworks after Ted's spectacular crash. Six long months of modeling, rendering, and animation were put in by the staff at Lamb & Co. to complete the first full-length, computer-generated cartoon.

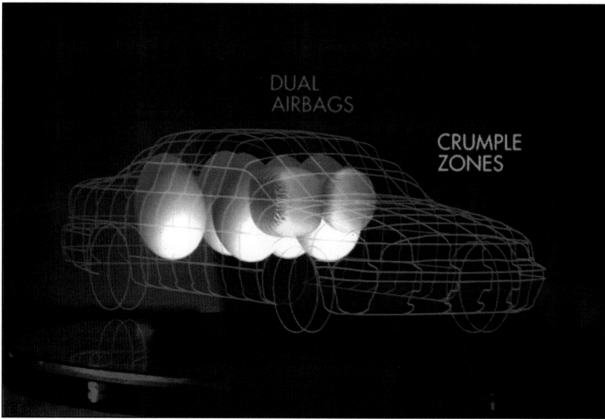

DUAL
AIRBAGS

CRUMPLE
ZONES

Courtesy of Grey Advertising and Rhythm & Hues.

This image from a Mitsubishi commercial illustrates that it is possible to see what is both inside and behind the computer wireframe image.

multiple characters, animators are often assigned to one particular character. This means they develop all the shots in which their character plays a part. When it shares the stage with another animator's character, the animators collaborate to create the scene. With this approach, animators can get to know their character's persona intimately and keep its behavior consistent throughout the entire production.

The second approach, most often used with shorter pieces, is simply to assign shots and scenes based on animator availability and shot order. Short format commercial spots do not need long-term character consistency, and so the needs of the production schedule and the availability of talent take precedence. In the case of "Crash Dummies," a combination of both was used. The primary characters had lead animators, but the overwhelming demands of producing 45,000 frames of animation on a tight production schedule often required using anybody else who might be available to help out.

Why Use Wireframe?

With wireframe images, the animator can see through to the other side of the object and so can often determine if it is intersecting with another surface. Wireframe also eases the burden on the computer by minimizing the number of calculations that must be performed to move the objects around on the screen. Keep in mind that every repositioning and every change of viewpoint requires the computer to recalculate the appearance of the objects presented. The fact that the animator can move objects in real time simply means that a very fast computer is computing the changes as they are being made.

Once a shot is assigned and the models built, the animators can begin. According to the needs of their shot, they call up on their monitor screen all the necessary props for that scene. These props are arranged according to the set design specified in the storyboard. Care must be taken that none of the objects occupy the same space. This is a basic law of the physical universe, and a law that generally applies to the world of animation as well. Unfortunately, the computer has no idea where the edges and surfaces are with respect to each other, and so the animator often must look at the set from several angles to determine whether all objects are properly separated.

In-betweens were used to fill in the action in this humorous tale of indigestion on an alien planet.

Moving the Character

Once the scene is set, the animator then specifies a motion path for the element being animated. This is the path the action will take. Similarly, the movement of the camera during the shot can be specified at this time. Since the animation camera is not real, it can fly and zoom around the set and capture the action in ways not possible with a physical camera. While the point of view of the animation camera is what will be used for the final recording of the shot, the animator can animate the scene from any point of view.

After specifying where the character is to move, the animator must define how it will move there. Will it roll? Will it stretch? Will it walk? These choices are character dependent and must be kept consistent with the type of world in which the story takes place. In general, the gross movements are specified first, followed by finer and finer detail. Thus, the body is moved first, followed by the legs and arms, followed by the feet and hands, and eventually the toes and fingers if necessary.

In this short film, Bill Reeves of Pixar created a simulation of a grassy field on a windy day. All the action of the film was controlled automatically by the computer.

Automatic Animation

The automatic generation of in-betweens raises the issue of whether the goal of computer animation is to automate the entire process. In other words, let the computer create the execution of a story. A vast amount of time and money has been spent creating visual simulations of real-world situations, such as curtains blowing or balls bouncing. Why not apply this approach to the world of animation?

While simulating reality is an admirable way to understand our reality better, moving computer animation in this direction loses sight of what animation is all about. Its purpose is to tell a story, nothing more. Its techniques, such as exaggeration and squash-and-stretch, have little, if anything, to do with the physics of the real world. Instead of reality, the animator wants to create a stylized believability that captures the essence of one or more human emotions. A computer will not be able to animate successfully on its own until it can think, feel, create, and have a sense of humor. Despite technological advances, this is still a long way off.

® Used with permission from Pillsbury.
Image courtesy of Pacific Data Images.

The low-resolution image of the Pillsbury Doughboy (top) was used to flesh out the animation for the Doughboy's "Mambo" commercial. After the client approved the animation, it was time for the final high-resolution rendering (right).

The Key Is Key-Framing

The motions are created through what is called key-framing. In any movement there are key points at which a motion component, like the raising of a knee, begins and ends. In between these points is a smooth interpolation of that movement. With key-framing, the animator need only create the starting and ending frames of the desired motion sequence. Based on the time that the movement should take, the animator then tells the computer

Through fear and fighting, life destroys itself in a dream vision shown during the *Luxor Live?* attraction at the Luxor Las Vegas Hotel.

to create a specific number of in-between frames called *in-betweens.*

The process of key framing came from traditional 2-D cel animation. There, the lead animator would draw the character in its key-frame positions, and a junior animator would then create the in-betweens. In this case, the junior animator has been replaced by the computer. Additionally, the computer animator does not have to "draw" the key frames. The objects being moved have a fixed 3-dimensional shape and are simply placed in the start and end positions. In a few seconds, the in-betweens are generated, and the animator can see whether it conveys the right action and emotion. If not, other movements can be tested immediately until the right one is discovered.

Virtually all animated movements are built up in this fashion, one key frame sequence at a time, until the full motion has been created. This includes everything from the gross movements of a character through the set, to the raise of an eyebrow or the smile of a mouth. Because of the flexibility of the digital environment, each of these moving elements can be viewed either on its own or in the broader context of the scene's entire action. Adding

detailed context can slow the computer's response, so an animator usually looks for an acceptable compromise between the two. For Example, PDI's animation system allows them to turn off the display of any scene elements they aren't directly working on. Later, they can turn these elements back on to test their animation in a fuller context.

Once the animation of a particular shot or scene is completed, a low-resolution version is created for client approval. If the animation has been created for compositing into live action, a digitized version of the live action is brought into the computer. The animation footage is then automatically inserted into the live action frame by frame.

With animation approval, work can then begin on its lighting and rendering.

Rendering: Let There Be Light!

The modeler provided form, the animator, life, yet the animation is still not complete. The creatures and objects created are but shadows or outlines of what they could be. They are hints of an evolving reality that has yet to be made solid and concrete.

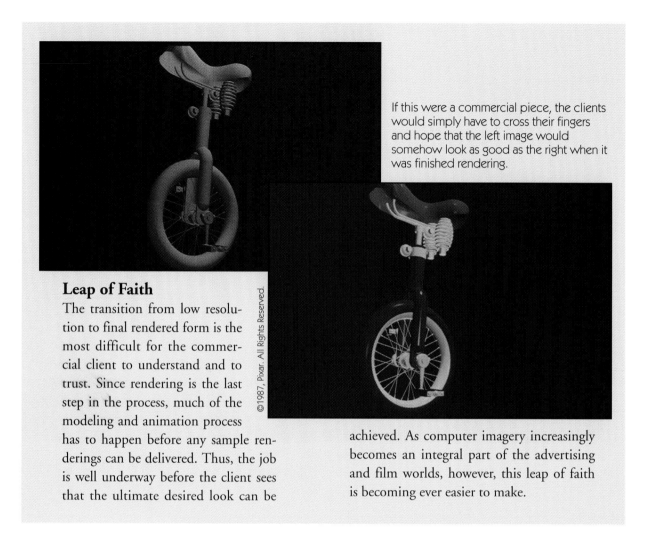

If this were a commercial piece, the clients would simply have to cross their fingers and hope that the left image would somehow look as good as the right when it was finished rendering.

Leap of Faith

The transition from low resolution to final rendered form is the most difficult for the commercial client to understand and to trust. Since rendering is the last step in the process, much of the modeling and animation process has to happen before any sample renderings can be delivered. Thus, the job is well underway before the client sees that the ultimate desired look can be achieved. As computer imagery increasingly becomes an integral part of the advertising and film worlds, however, this leap of faith is becoming ever easier to make.

Up to this point, animators and modelers have been working in either wire-frame representations or with low resolution, shaded objects. Neither of these representations looks anything like the way the final product will appear. At low resolution, surfaces generally look faceted or bumpy, colors have very little subtlety, and dramatic lighting is missing entirely.

Modelers and animators work with wireframe and low resolution imagery for two principle reasons. The first is one of priority. To the modeler, the object's final look is not as important as its underlying structure; and to the animator, the object's movements are what really count. The second is that high-resolution rendering is very expensive in terms of computer time. A single complex frame can often require hours of dedicated number crunching on even the fastest computer. To attempt to animate or model at this resolution would be impossible.

Rendering is the most computationally demanding phase of the entire animation process. Modeling a complex element can often take weeks of work, but once a model is created, it can be used repeatedly in any number of scenes. Rendering, on the other hand, is largely a frame-by-frame process. Just because the same model appears in two successive frames of animation, it does not necessarily save time. If the computer camera has moved even the slightest bit, the entire frame must be re-rendered. What's more, all the specified surfaces of every object, even those that are not seen, are rendered in each frame. This is because there is no easy way to selectively render what has changed, and because the colors, lights, and shadows of the various invisible parts often affect the appearance of what is seen.

The Rendering Process

During rendering, the computer does virtually all the work using software that has either been purchased off the shelf or developed by in-house programmers. Human intervention is needed only if the software runs into difficulty. In this case, the machine with the problem image signals a programmer, who attempts to correct either the rendering software or the faulty specifications of the image being generated. Lamb & Co., during their "Crash Dummies" production, used the sound of breaking glass to alert the programming staff to problems. If there were no difficulties, however, their machines lowed like contented cows.

The process of rendering is far more than just painting a picture on a computer screen or a frame of film. Essentially, for any image rendered, the computer must first build a 3-dimensional world, then paint it and light it, and finally "photograph" it from the perspective of the computer camera.

Working from a digital file that represents the frame being rendered, the computer first assembles and positions all the elements that make up the frame. In the final rendering stage, these elements are usually calculated at very high resolutions in order to eliminate the jagged appearance of any curved surfaces or lines.

After the elements have been built, the computer then creates their surfaces by applying the specified surface maps or colors to the appropriate parts of the objects. This involves a series of complex computations to determine the exact configuration of the surfaces.

Next, the objects are lighted. Using stored information about the number of lights on the set, their type, their strength and color, and their direction, the computer then begins to create the lighting effects. The look of the lighting is affected by the surfaces of the objects, the types of lights specified, and the mathematical models used to calculate the behavior of light.

Once the lighting has been completed, it is now time to create what the camera sees. Keep in mind that in the world just constructed, all the objects have tops, sides, bottoms, and possibly insides. To determine what is visible, the computer must now take into consideration the type of lens on the imaginary camera, the effects of any atmospheric filters such as smoke and haze, and the speed at which any of the elements or the camera is moving. Motion information is needed to create what is called motion blur, which occurs when a fast moving object passes before a camera with its shutter open.

To create the final 2-D image, the computer then scans the resulting 3-D world and pulls out only the pixels the camera can see. The rest is discarded. This set of visible pixels is then sent to the monitor, to videotape, or to a film recorder for display.

Surface Maps

In computer graphics, it is possible to take any 2-dimensional image and attach it to any 3-dimensional surface. This is called surface mapping, and it can be used to glue texture, pattern, or any kind of imagery to a computer-generated object. It can even be used to attach successive frames of video or film, so the object carries with it a moving picture.

Lighting in the Dark

Lighting a computer-generated scene is one of the most difficult tasks in computer graphics. While the lighting

This entire stadium (the lights, grass, and spectators) was created on computer for the Anheuser-Busch "Bud Bowl" advertising campaign. Final rendering created the shadows, the highlights around the stadium lights, the varied color of the field, and the colors of thousands of computer-generated spectators.

Reprinted with permission by Anheuser-Busch Company.

designer can easily specify things like the number of light sources needed, their intensities, their colors, and a wide selection of other behavioral parameters, it is not possible to see the full results without a high-resolution rendering of it.

Where an animator or modeler can correct a mistake interactively, lighting designers often have to wait hours to see the results of their efforts. If their choices were wrong, they have to make another guess and hope for the best. The process has been likened to lighting a live-action set in the dark. First, all the lights are turned off. Then the lighting designer runs around to each light, aims it, inserts the colored gels, and sets its intensity. Finally, the lights are turned back on to check the results. If they aren't what was hoped for, the whole process is repeated.

Because of the expense of final rendering, lighting decisions for entire scenes are often made on the basis of one or two high-resolution frames per scene. If the lighting works in those frames, it is assumed that it will work in all the others. Even for the most experienced lighting designers, however, this can sometimes create unexpected results. With complex sets, it is easy to overlook shadows or dark areas where the light does not reach. And if part of the action happens to move through one of these areas, it will disappear, thus ruining the scene.

Fortunately, when this occurs it is often not necessary to re-render the whole scene. The lighting designer can simply "cheat" the lighting specifications in the problem frames by adding new light sources to brighten the dark

areas. Only those frames are then sent back to the renderer.

Cheat the Light Fantastic

"Cheaters never prosper" is an adage that will never apply to computer graphics lighting designers. They cheat all the time, both because they want to and because they have to. They want to because cheating in visual productions represents control, and control is of paramount importance to achieving the desired effects. They have to because computer lights do not behave the way lights do in the real world.

Computer lights, being digital, are completely under the lighting designers' control. Designers can specify whether those lights will cast shadows or not; they can select which objects in any scene each light will illuminate; and since the light sources themselves are invisible, they can place them anywhere in the set without blocking anything else from sight. In addition, lights can be made to shine through the seeming solidity of walls, floors, or any other object. Pixar used this technique in *Tin Toy* to light the baby after it had fallen to the floor, and make it seem as if the light were reflecting from the floor itself.

The End is in Sight

Despite how far computer graphics technology has come, creating a computer animation requires a large amount of very dedicated effort. All three major steps in the process

This huge interior space required 16 separate computer lights to light it properly. Even though only three of those lights actually cast shadows, it seems as if all the lights do.

Here, Tinny the tin toy is about to run in terror from the baby in Pixar's film, *Tin Toy*. Notice the four-paned window highlight on his face and side. This is a "cheat" shined directly on him.

demand the full attention of the animators involved because absolutely everything that is to appear on-screen must be meticulously planned and executed.

Once rendering is completed, the work is almost done. The tasks remaining fall into what is called post production. During this phase, the various live-action and computer graphics elements are composited together, the final sound track is dubbed in, and various 2-D paint effects are added. Once this is complete, the final piece is sent to videotape for television broadcast or to a film recorder to be captured on film.

Previsualization: You Can See It Before You See It

Computer visualization, the process of using the computer to create images of products before they are built or of events that can't easily be seen with the naked eye, has revolutionized virtually every area of science and engineering in which it has been used. Through visual computer-based simulations, researchers at the National Bureau of Standards Fire Safety Department can safely study how fire spreads through a closed room. Scientists at Johns Hopkins can test how a recovering patient might walk after a skeletal operation before the operation takes place. Engineers at Boeing can build and test-fly new jet designs before the ore for the plane's body is even mined from the ground. This ability to see the results of an experiment, medical operation, or product design on computer, before committing to a course of action, has greatly increased both safety and the likelihood of successful results.

Courtesy of Mazda Motor of America.

The Mazda "Time Capsule" television spot was previsualized by Rhythm & Hues well before any of the set was built.

Rhythm & Hues used previsualization in its production of Grey Advertising's "Mitsubishi Magnifying Glass" television spot, not only to determine the optimal movement of the camera and the magnifying loop, but also to create the construction plans for building the loop itself.

With the growing improvement of computer-image quality, this process of visualization also promises to revolutionize the visual arts. Increasingly, filmmakers and commercial directors are turning to computer graphics to help them see their ideas on-screen before they create them in the real world. They are finding that the preview process, or previsualization as it is called, is saving them both time and money, and in the end, helping to create better products on tighter production schedules.

The Mind's Eye and Motion Control

While previsualization in the entertainment industry is still in its infancy, its roots stretch back to the year 1978. It was at this time that Robert Abel & Associates, a Clio-award-winning design studio in Los Angeles, purchased one of the first commercially available visual computing systems to preview the movements of their motion control devices.

Motion control devices are digitally driven camera mounts that automatically direct a camera's movements around a model or live-action set. Many special effects for both film and television use elaborate models to produce an effect. For example, Director Arish Fyzee supervises the programming of a motion-control camera move for the "Theatre of Time" for the Luxor Las Vegas Hotel while a video monitor (not shown) shows what the camera sees. In the background, the VistaVision ™ camera attached to

the gantry hangs in the middle of the miniature set. The curved lines on the computer monitor specify how the camera will slow and accelerate as it moves through the model.

The primary advantage of motion-control devices over live-action filming is that since they are computer controlled, their movements are precisely repeatable, something that is not possible when a human operates a camera. This allows the repeated layering of new effects on each pass of the camera. One of the difficulties with motion-control devices, however, is determining beforehand what the optimal camera path through the set might be. There are simply too many variables for the mind to keep track of. The director may initially have a particular approach in mind, but at time of shooting may find that a different path works better.

Changing a camera's path can wreak havoc on a set because it is often not just a matter of simply changing where the camera moves. Models are usually built with specific camera motions in mind and so to change the move can require expensive rebuilding of parts of the model. In addition, the actual shooting may reveal that some parts of the model need greater detail, or that parts of the miniatures are lining up oddly and creating distracting visual patterns.

Without computer previsualization, visual artifacts such as these are very difficult to notice. Finding the right motion on one's own can often require several expensive test runs and model rebuilds, wasting film and time and running the risk of damaging the set itself. Previsualization, although not perfect, can drastically reduce live-action repeats, and it can also, on occasion, catch errors that might not otherwise have been caught until well into the production process.

For Robert Abel & Associates this proved true shortly after they bought their first visualization system. In one particular Levi's advertisement, the camera was to travel across the set and eventually pass between the legs of a workman using a jackhammer. Their previsualization showed them that everything looked great until the commercial's key moment when the camera passed between the man's legs. Here they noticed a slight distortion of the camera's view because of the lens they were using, something that would never have been detected until after the scene had been shot. Instead, they were able to compensate ahead of time by using a different camera lens, thus saving themselves the expense of reshooting the scene.

Controlling the Future, Today

Today, computer previsualization has expanded well beyond its initial association with motion control. It is used not only to specify camera moves, but also to create storyboards, design sets, and preview action scenes as well. Rhythm & Hues, a prominent Los Angeles computer graphics studio, makes extensive use of computer previewing in almost all of its commercial productions. In fact, previsualization information often controls the entire development, from start to finish, of many of their productions.

The first step at Rhythm & Hues, once they receive the client's storyboard, is to build a detailed computer model of the set and all its props. To determine the scale, they first construct a digital model of the featured product. The rest of the set is then built in relation to that element. For example, in their Mazda "Time Capsule" ad created by Foote, Cone & Belding, they constructed a computer model of the Mazda MX-6 first. Then, they built the tube into which the car was to fit and the detailed warehouse setting that was to surround it all.

Using their models, they then explored how to move the camera and the primary elements, in order to show the Mazda MX-6 to advantage while not crashing into any of the props. In complex sets, where both camera and scene elements are moving at the same time, finding an unobstructed path is often difficult. Testing possible scenarios on a computer allows the production team to discover

Motion-control camera for "Theatre of Time" at Luxor Hotel.

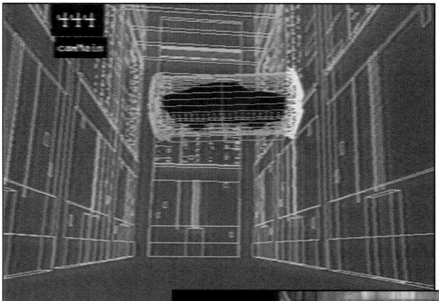

The entire Mazda "Time Capsule" television spot was previsualized by Rhythm & Hues well before any of the set was built. Here, we see a wireframe previsualization test of the crane moving the Mazda MX-6 first through the warehouse.

Courtesy of Mazda Motor of America.

This image from the final commercial footage shows the exact same scene as the previous picture, showing how close the previsualization process is to the ultimate product.

where the problems are before building them into the set.

Getting Physical

Once the digital set and camera motion look right, it is time to get physical. Keep in mind that not a single prop has yet been constructed for the live-action stage. Creating printed specifications for each set prop, however, is just a simple process of extracting the data from the computer model, printing the plans, and giving them to the construction crew.

When the real set is complete, filming can begin. As a result of the early digital tests, the motion path for the camera is already in the computer. This information is fed to the motion control system and presto, out comes an instant commercial. Well, almost. Actually, the motion data is rarely perfect, and minor changes to the physical camera's path usually have to be made. These changes, in turn, are captured by the computer controlling the motion rig and then fed back to the computer model.

This is extremely useful for the later addition of computer graphics effects. For these to be believable, they must fit into the live action very precisely. If the movement of the live-action camera and the computer camera are not in synch, the results will be disastrous. Once they have been matched, however, effects like reflections on the car windows or feature transformations, can be composited in exactly the right spot in the live-action footage.

Seeing the Future in Films

Due to uncertainties about image quality, cost, and speed, the use of computer graphics in film has always lagged behind its application in commercial work. The incorporation of previsualization in filmmaking is no exception to this rule. While it is beginning to control many commercial productions from start to finish, it is only just finding its place in feature films.

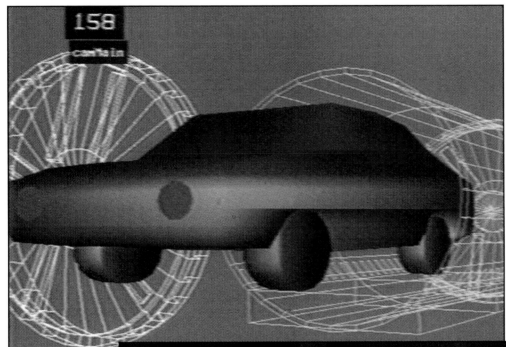

In another scene from the Mazda "Time Capsule" television spot, Rhythm & Hues used a low-resolution computer model of the Mazda to visualize the action as the car was placed inside the time capsule.

The same scene as above, taken from the final footage, shows the MX-6 backing into the capsule. The capsule top is entirely computer generated, while the platform on which it sits is a stage prop built according to the previsualization specifications.

Courtesy of Mazda Motor of America.

The first film director to make extensive use of computer visualization in a major feature was James Cameron. In his 1989 film, *The Abyss*, he employed computer graphics not only to create the watery pseudopod special effect, but also to produce storyboards, design sets, and develop many of the expensive miniature models for the underwater shots. None of these uses, however, involved previsualizing live-action scenes. The computer operated more like a computer-aided design (CAD) workstation than as a window on the future.

The Chase Is On

With the formation in 1993 of Sony Pictures Imageworks (SPI) and its previsualization group, however, this is all changing. Directors are now discovering that computer graphics is more than just a special effects tool and can also be used to preview and plan expensive and dangerous live-action shots. For example, In the Columbia Picture's film, *Striking Distance*, starring Bruce Willis, director Rowdy Herrington used SPI's previsualization group to simulate the opening chase scene. From this, they were able to test camera angles and lenses, and specify exactly how and where each stunt should take place all before any film was shot.

The scene called for a high-speed tunnel chase in heavy traffic and a close-up shot of a police cruiser flipping over and skidding along on its roof. Filming a stunt like this is never easy and requires meticulous planning. Mistakes in camera placement, lens selection, or stunt timing can mean expensive reshooting as well as increased likelihood of injury. To create the simulation, SPI's previsualization group began by building a digital model of the tunnel. Since the stunt was to be filmed in Pittsburgh, they used construction data from the city's planning office to give them the tunnel's dimensions.

To produce the tunnel's interior, video footage was shot of the real tunnel and surrounding streets and then mapped onto the computer model. The vehicles, which included taxis, buses, police cars, and more were either modeled from scratch or purchased from an existing 3-D library. Once all the elements were in place, the vehicles

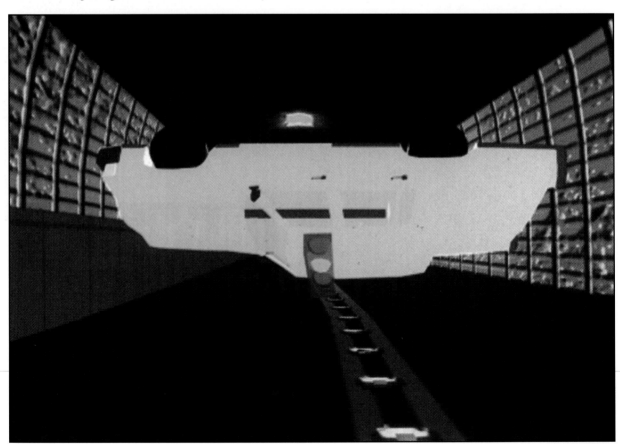

For Columbia Picture's action film, *Striking Distance*, Sony Pictures Image Works used previsualization to preplan a complex and dangerous chase scene and tunnel crash.

The live action for *Striking Distance* turned out to look almost exactly like the previsualization tests.

were set in motion. Initial views of the simulation were shot from overhead by removing the digital roof of the tunnel. This allowed the stunt coordinator to work out precisely where he wanted the police car to swerve into the killer's car and start to flip.

Once the action was set, they then used the simulation to test various camera angles and lenses, mounting one camera on the side of one car and another on top of the police car lights. After several tests, they were able to determine what best captured the scene. From here, it was simply a matter of translating the simulation data to the real world. Since the models of all the elements matched the real setting exactly, the director could lay out precisely where and when each stunt was to take place. The result was a perfectly executed and photographed sequence that came out looking amazingly like the computer previsualization.

Motion Control: Robots in Film

The dynamite explodes and the careening gasoline truck bursts into flame. A burning figure fights its way out of the inferno that was the cab. The figure stumbles, falls, and the fire claims it. Safe at last, the hero and heroine turn to leave, but the harsh sound of metal tearing and shifting behind them spins them back to the wreckage. Slowly and deliberately, up from the flames rises a horrifying, blue-metal skeleton. The chase continues.

When we think of robots in film, images of strange science fiction creatures come to mind: the comical rubber-armed tin can from the *Lost In Space* television series, the stiff-legged, sheet-metal skinned Klatu in the film *The Day The Earth Stood Still*, or the terrifying blue-metal skeleton and his liquid alloy sequel in both *The Terminator* and *Terminator 2: Judgment Day*.

While these are just figments of the various directors' imaginations, there are, in fact, real robots in films, and they are responsible for a very important part of the filmmaking process. Without them, many of the special effects that capture our imaginations would not be possible. They are the gears and circuitry that make up what are called motion-control devices.

The Trumbull Company's giant motion-control gantry system looms over one of the miniature sets for "The Theatre of Time" created for the Luxor Las Vegas Hotel.

A VistaVision™ camera attached to the Trumbull Company's motion-control gantry hovers over a miniature set for "The Theatre of Time."

Funny, You Don't Look Like a Robot...

Motion-control rigs are computer-controlled boom arms and gantry supports that move a camera along a preset path through a live-action or miniature-model set. They look nothing like the animated, semi-sentient mechanical beings pictured in films. They are designed purely for one function and that is moving the camera as precisely as possible through a given space.

Booms

The most common approach is to mount the camera on a swiveling platform attached to the end of a boom arm. The boom arm looks much like the industrial robots used to manufacture automobiles. The base of the boom, which can swivel, extend, and move vertically, is attached to a movable bed normally set on metal tracks. Therefore, the device can roll across a stage while extending, raising, and rotating the arm, at the end of which is a rotating and swiveling camera. The camera itself operates as any normal camera and so can focus and zoom during the action.

Motion-control booms are extremely flexible, but they are also limited. The primary problem lies in the overall stability of the resulting structure. Since it is of paramount importance that all the camera motions be exactly measurable and precisely repeatable, any momentary vibrations or extraneous movements must be eliminated. If they are not, the extra motion will make it very difficult to synchronize multiple camera passes over the same scene. Wherever these passes are composited together, the viewer will notice blurred or fuzzy edges or perhaps even gross mismatches in the film imagery.

Moving Through the Past

While modern motion-control technology is intimately tied to the digital computer, the first experiments in automatic camera control took place in the 1940s just after World War II. Filmmaker and visual artist, John Whitney, Sr., wanted a new method for controlling the frame-by-frame, stop-motion animation techniques of his day. These frame-at-a-time approaches, used in King Kong and other early monster movies, created jerky, unrealistic movements and he wanted greater fluidity.

The digital computer was only then being born and was not available for anything but scientific experimentation. Instead, Whitney used a discarded analog controller that had been used during World War II for sighting artillery. His experiments at this time, unfortunately, were largely failures because the analog nature of the controller did not give him the precise digital control he needed. His work did, however, serve as a model for the digitally based systems when they came into use in the 1970s.

Errors in the motion system start to creep in as the boom arm grows in size. Because of the basic physics of rigid structures, the longer the arm the more unstable its movement. Even with extra reinforcement and the use of extremely stiff materials, the largest motion-control boom in use has only a 40-foot reach.

> Analog refers to a type of electrical signal. It is smooth and continuous, while a digital signal is made up of strings of separate pulses.

Gantries

To deal with motion over a larger area, it is necessary to build what is called a gantry. Most of us are more accustomed to hearing this word in connection with space exploration. The structure that holds the Space Shuttle or any rocket in place before launch is called a gantry. A gantry, however, is any rigid structure used to provide stability to various objects. In this case the object is a movie camera.

Motion-control gantries look like the giant shipyard cranes used to unload container ships. In shipyards, two outside struts support a beam between them on which a crane can move up and down or side to side. For filmwork, the crane is replaced with a movable camera mount that can swivel, extend, and tilt in any direction. The base of each strut is set on a track, allowing the entire gantry to move.

Created by Ketchum Advertising and executed by George Lucas' Industrial Light & Magic (ILM), this spot required matching live action of the 1994 Acura Integra speeding along a "Hot Wheels" ramp, with motion control footage of a 1/8th scale model of the car and track.

Courtesy of Ketchum Advertising and Industrial Light & Magic.

The Trumbull Company's giant motion-control gantry system looms over one of the miniature sets for "The Theatre of Time" created for the Luxor Las Vegas Hotel.

The largest gantry built to date was constructed by The Trumbull Company for the Luxor Hotel project described in detail in Chapter 17, "Luxor Hotel." It can move the full length of the company's 200 foot warehouse at speeds up to 6 feet per second and stop within 3/1000ths of an inch of its target destination.

Regardless of whether the motion-control rig is a boom, a gantry, or any other device, they are all designed to be controlled by computer. All of the movable joints, wheels, gears, and internal camera controls are rigged with sensors that measure their precise movements, as well as motors to move them. The sensors function as either senders or receivers, depending on how the camera is being used.

Digital Do-Si-Do

Motion-control cameras operate in two primary ways. They either receive motion data from a computer and move accordingly, or they capture this same information from the moving rig and relay it back to the computer for storage and later replay. The cameras, however, are almost never used exclusively in one mode or the other during a production, but provide a handy feedback tool for refining and redesigning automated camera moves.

In the preceding chapter, we saw that camera paths through live-action sets can be specified by first creating

Moving Heaven and Earth

As motion-control technology has developed, it has moved from controlling only the movement of the camera to moving the models being filmed as well. It is now possible to specify a motion path for the camera and a series of movements for the object being filmed. In the feature film, *Captain Ron*, this is exactly what was done to create the tossing of the ship in a stormy sea.

The model of the ship was mounted on a pedestal. The computer-controlled mount pitched and yawed like a ship in high seas, while fans blew its sails. The motion-control camera then moved around the toy ship, shooting it against blue screen (for further details, see Chapter 7, "The Door Between

Two Worlds: Embedding 3-D in Live Action"). The final film frames were created by pasting live footage of an empty, stormy sea around the ship.

This form of motion control, called "Go Motion," grew out of George Lucas' filming of the *Star Wars* series. Stop motion is the frame-by-frame animation technique used in films like *King Kong* to move miniature models of the giant ape. In stop motion, the model is moved between frames. The resulting motion is somewhat jerky and barely believable by today's standards. Go motion, on the other hand, moves the model while the camera shutter is still open. This creates what is called motion blur and a sense of more fluid movement.

digital models of the sets. A computer camera is then moved around inside these sets until the best path is found. The resulting three-dimensional data that defines that path inside the computer-generated environment is what is used to choreograph the real camera on stage. If the actual set is built to the specifications of the computer model, then the previewed motion will work. If the likeness is not exact, from the size of the objects to their precise placement on the stage, the camera may end up bumping into something, much like misstepping partners in a square dance.

The Other Way Around

Often, however, it is neither possible nor desirable to use digital previewing to specify the camera moves. Strict digital preplanning can restrict the director's creativity by forcing him or her to comply to the preset camera motion. Similarly, there are situations, such as when shots must be filmed outside of the controlled environment of a sound stage, where the live action has to be filmed first.

Here, the director relies on the motion-control device itself to capture the needed information. In this case, the camera person simply shoots the scene, and the sensors on the rig record the precise motion by sending it to the attached computer. Once the information is recorded, it can be played back through the rig to repeat exactly the entire move created by the camera person.

Why Go to All This Trouble?

Motion-control rigs are difficult to build, expensive, and sometimes finicky to operate. The slightest error in any one of their components can make them unreliable. With these difficulties, why bother? What use is an exactly repeatable camera move, anyway?

This goes to the heart of special effects production. Most special effects are built up through a layering process, called compositing, in which successive photographic elements, such as explosions, spaceships, or alien creatures, for example, are added to a given set of frames. These effects elements are almost always separately photographed or created in computer imagery, because it

Photos of car transformation to tiger compliments of Exxon Company, USA, ©Exxon Corp. 1994.

The car for this Exxon advertisement executed by Pacific Data Images (PDI) was shot using a camera under the control of a camera man and was captured by the computer for subsequent passes of the camera.

Without a motion-control camera, it would have been extremely difficult to remove the straw portions protruding above the glasses and replace them with computer-generated and animated straws. For further details see Chapter 12 "Fresca, 'Chuckling Straws.'"

would be too difficult, dangerous, or perhaps even impossible to capture them all in a single photographic session.

Breaking It into Pieces

Successful filmmaking depends on breaking scenes down into their elemental parts and filming these alone. This minimizes the number of things that can go wrong and ruin a shot. After each part of a shot has been captured on film, then it can be combined with the others to form the entire image.

Combining them properly demands meticulous frame-by-frame matching of the various shots to the live-action footage. This, in turn, requires that the camera and all the associated objects in that set of frames move in exactly the same way no matter how many times the sequence is shot. Only digital control of both the cam-

A "distopian" view of the future from the Luxor Las Vegas Hotel's "Theatre of Time". Although the motion gantry developed by the Trumbull Company for their model shots was perhaps the most accurate in the world, it still had a small amount of error in its movements that had to be accounted for in order to properly embed the computer graphic airships and people into scenes of the future.

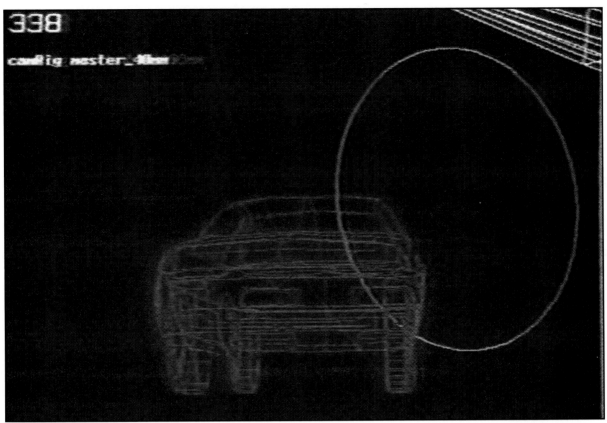

Courtesy of Grey Advertising and Rhythm & Hues.

Rhythm & Hues first specified the motion of the camera and the magnifying glass in its spot Mitsubishi "Magnifying Glass" for Grey Advertising. They then took those motion paths and used them to pilot the live action motion-control rigs onstage.

era and the moving objects offers this level of repeatability. Once a motion path has been specified as a series of exact digital numbers, there is very little room for errors to creep in.

You Mean Even Computers Make Mistakes?

Despite its infinite repeatability, motion-control systems are not always exactly correct. Even with the Trumbull Company's gantry, precise to within 3/1000ths of an inch, errors can occur. For example, if there are seven moving gears and wheels that are used to create a specific motion, it is possible that the final position of the camera can be off by the sum of each element's tolerance. Thus, the camera could think it is pointing at one spot when it is really slightly off to the side.

This is what Kleiser-Walczak Construction Co. found during the production of computer imagery for the Trumbull Company's Luxor Hotel project. When they went to match the digital spaceships they created to the live-action model footage shot on the Trumbull stage, the two shots could not be synchronized exactly. To rectify the problem, technicians at Kleiser-Walczak took extensive measurements of the physical camera and compared those to the motion-control data captured by that camera. By taking literally hundreds of separate measurements, they eventually figured out how and why the real camera varied from the data. This fluctuation was then built into their computer camera making an exact match.

Well Worth the Trouble

Digital motion-control systems are not 100% perfect, but they have given the filmmaker and the commercial director an unprecedented level of control over their final products. With these systems, special effects that combine live action, model movements, and computer graphics are not only possible but have become regular additions to feature films and television commercials. For the foreseeable future, it is only likely that their uses and applications will expand as digital technology makes further inroads into the visual arts.

Performance Animation and Synthetic Actors

Are You For Real?

The theater is silent. The live audience watching George Coates' new play, "Box Conspiracy," has just heard the charges and the evidence against the defendant, Isabel Hornsby. It is time for a verdict. On the movie screen backstage, behind the celebrity emcee for this episode of the Home Jury Duty Channel, the face of Judge Mike appears. "I declare the defendant, not guilty!" he pronounces and then promptly disappears. Derek Hornsby, Isabel's mild-mannered husband and part-time media terrorist, quickly hides the hand-held computer he has used to manipulate the Judge. The astonished emcee sees nothing as she turns back. The audience, however, realizes it has just witnessed another in a series of Derek's humorous high-tech media-jackings.

Moxy, the Cartoon Network's digital mascot, can be performed live by an actor wearing a motion-capture suit.

George Coates, renowned San Francisco performance artist, combines technology and art to create some of the most captivating works in modern theater. In the above scene from his 1993 work, "Box Conspiracy: An Interactive Shō," Judge Mike is no mere human actor. He is a 3-D computer image animated in real time for every performance.

> Real time refers to the time we all experience every day. If something happens in real time, it happens as we are watching it.

And just as Judge Mike was making his debut in West Coast theater, the first live television performance of a 3-D computer character was taking place in the East. On the day after Thanksgiving 1993, Moxy, a manic digital dog, appeared as the new emcee and mascot for CNN's Cartoon Network. He performed hourly throughout the day, and his antics were broadcast live over worldwide cable television.

How is this possible? Can computer animation, the product of such a long, laborious and detailed process actually be performed live? The answer to this is both yes and no. The high-resolution characters created for feature films and television commercials still cannot be animated in real time. There is simply too much data to move around and too little time to move it. However, with the ever-increasing speed and power of current computer hardware and software, live performance is becoming possible for lower-resolution, less complex imagery.

The Live and Not-So-Live

Performance animation actually encompasses more than just the real-time animations its name implies. It also includes what are called synthetic actors. Synthetic actors are computer graphic models of both humanoid and cartoon characters that use the movements of real humans to create their motions but do not move in real time. The reason they are still considered to be part of performance animation and not simply part of the more standard

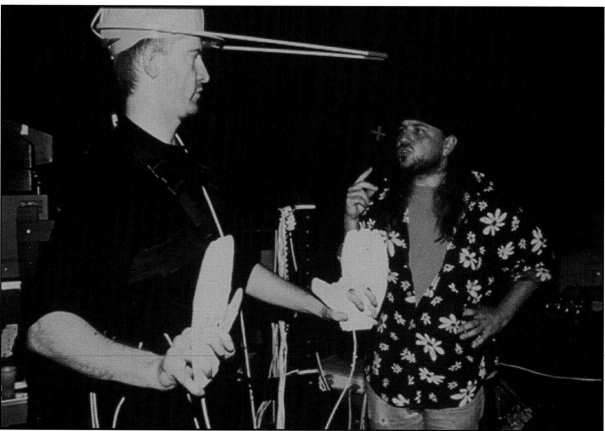

Courtesy of Colossal Pictures. "Moxy" produced by Colossal Pictures in association with the Cartoon Network.

Actor John Stevenson wears a magnetic-based motion-control harness as he and comedian Bobcat Goldthwait perform Moxy's movements and voice. Each cable attached to Stevenson is connected to a motion sensor mounted strategically on his body.

A selection of sculpted expressions for Nestor Sextone. These masks were digitized into the computer and served as a set of key frame positions for animating Nestor's face.

key-frame approach is that their movements are, in fact, the result of a real-time performance.

Actors wearing various hardware devices often referred to as waldos, move about on-stage while the devices track their movements. These movements are captured in real time by computer. For live performances, the actor is hidden from the audience, and these movements are transferred directly to the computer image. For the not-so-live, they are captured and stored for later application to the character's computer graphic image. In either case, the capture process is extremely interactive, and the actor can see his or her movements immediately affect the character. With such direct feedback, it is possible to create the movements for an entire animation sequence in minutes versus hours (or even days) using the standard key-frame approach.

Despite its obvious benefits, however, performance-based animation can by no means replace the more traditional methods. For example, since it can capture only the movements that are actually made by a physical actor, it is not terribly useful for telling the wide range of stories that make up classic animation. Physical arms and legs simply do not squash,

Created by Kleiser-Walczak Construction Co., Nestor Sextone, the real world's first synthetic actor, is shown here campaigning for the presidency of the Synthetic Actor's Guild.

Dozo's movements were captured as singer Perla Betaila sang and danced before the microphone. Betaila's movements were then attached to Dozo's computer body.

video, and finally, on stage in 1993.

During this five-year period, several other more fully developed characters have joined him. There is Nestor Sextone, Dozo, Waldo C. Graphic, Lotta Desire, Moxy, and more. Some, such as Mike and Moxie, are real time actors, and others, such as Waldo and Dozo, simply use human motion to give them a greater sense of realism.

The Kleiser-Walczak Construction Co. has specialized in synthetic actors since the company's beginning in 1987. Their stable of actors now consists of Nestor Sextone, the muscular president of the Synthetic Actors Guild, Dozo, a female singer of multi-ethic background, and a cast of dancers and extras who performed in one of the films created for the Las Vegas Luxor Hotel.

stretch, or vibrate the way cartoon characters require them to. These types of stories are still best produced by hand because of the control an animator needs to exercise over the imagery.

> Key framing is the process by which an animator specifies the action in every third or fifth frame of a scene, for example, and the computer automatically fills in the missing frames.

Building the Synthetic Universe

The world of performance animation and synthetic actors is only a few years old. Judge Mike, who normally goes by the name of "Mike the Talking Head," is the oldest such character. He was born in 1988, matured quickly, and was used that same year to emcee the SIGGRAPH film and video show. To date, he has appeared on television, at selected business conferences, in an Australian Rock

Life from a Lump of Clay

To create a synthetic actor, Diana Walczak (co-founder of Kleiser-Walczak Construction Co.) begins by sculpting a scale model in clay. Sextone, being the first, was the most difficult of all. He required thirty-seven separate body parts, plus a series of over twenty-five facial expressions. Each part was created separately because at that time, computer animation software was not yet sophisticated enough to animate complex interlinked objects. Fortunately, the needed software has since been developed. Both Dozo and the dancers created for the Luxor Hotel were sculpted as single units.

Once the physical model is complete, it is then digitized with a 3-D magnetic digitizer. As explained earlier in the book, this creates a wireframe computer model ready to be brought to life. The next step is to capture the motion data from a live human actor. For Dozo, this meant hiring a singer and having her perform the music. As she sang, they used an optical tracking system to capture her movements. These movements were later attached to the

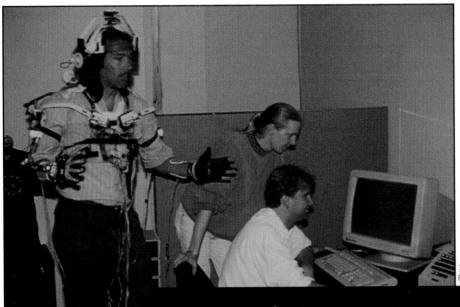

Jamie Dixon of Pacific Data Images wears their exo-skeleton motion capture harness as he performs the various parts of the skeletons in the 20th Century Fox film, *Toys*.

The green, luminescent skeletons in the film *Toys* do battle using Jamie Dixon's movements shown being captured above.

appropriate parts of her wireframe model. In addition to the captured motion for her body, they also had to animate Dozo's face. For this, they used the more traditional manual approach as well as lip-synch software they had developed for Sextone.

> A magnetic 3-D digitizer is a device that uses magnetic fields to create a 3-dimensional computer model from an existing real object.

With all this in place, they then rendered each frame of the action and captured them all on film. The result was a powerful music video and the world's first computer graphics rock star.

Motion Capture: Harnessing Human Movement

Motion capture, the process by which human motion is collected from the body of a live actor, lies at the heart of performance animation. Without motion capture, the liquid-alloy T1000 in *Terminator 2* would not have been nearly so terrifying. Capturing actor Robert Patrick's individual style of walking made a direct and unmistakable connection between the silver-skinned T1000 and Patrick's human form. Thus, the audience could more easily accept the superhuman powers of his seemingly benign policeman's appearance.

Similarly, without motion capture, the comical skeleton fight in the movie *Toys* would not have been so humorous. As the fight develops, the point of view flips between a group of aging generals fighting in their underwear and images of their skeletons in the same fight. The skeleton shots are closely intercut with the underwear shots so that the audience knows they are seeing two different views of the exact same scene. If the movements of the computer-generated skeletons had not matched the human generals, the humor would have been lost.

Courtesy of Carolco © 1991.

Using projected light as a guide, Make-up Artist Steven E. Anderson pencils a heavy black grid onto actor Robert Patrick's body.

Other studios prefer the more formalized optical approach developed by Motion Analysis in Santa Rosa, CA. Their system uses a battery of six high-speed video cameras that are stationed around the actor at specific intervals, and that record at the rate of 200 frames per second. The performer wears a series of highly reflective ping-pong balls taped to various points on the body, such as the knees, wrists, hips, head, and so on. Once the actor starts moving, the cameras relay their data to a set of powerful image processors, which calculates the exact coordinates of each ball at any point in time.

Creating human motions by computer is still extremely difficult for the standard key-frame approach. There are just too many subtle variations to specify manually on a frame-by-frame basis. Yet, it is precisely these subtleties that make human motions believable. The human eye is so accustomed to them that when these subtle variations are missing, the movements immediately look fake. To overcome this difficulty, several different approaches to capturing real human motion have been developed using optical, magnetic, and mechanical technologies.

Seeing Is Grabbing

The optical methods, as might be expected, are primarily visual. They generally use high speed video or film cameras trained on an actor to track his or her movements. The actor wears some sort of reference grid or reflective material that makes it easier to track the movements of specific body parts.

In the case of Robert Patrick, he was filmed by two cameras set at right angles. His body was covered with a heavy black grid of lines that later helped animators extract his movements. Using this approach, Industrial Light & Magic, George Lucas's special effects house, was able to incorporate Patrick's slight limp from an early sports injury into the T1000's walk, making the robot's movements look extremely realistic.

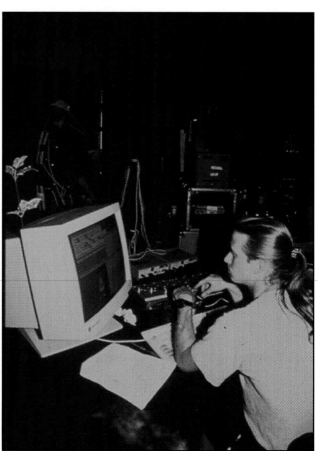

Moxy's finer facial movements are added by a member of Colossal Picture's effects team, using a pair of joystick-type waldos and a computer keyboard.

"Moxy" produced by Colossal Pictures in association with the Cartoon Network.

The advantage of using an optical approach over other forms of motion capture is that performers have more freedom of movement. They are not constrained by the often heavy or bulky hardware used in other motion capture systems. The down-side is that the system can confuse one reflective ball with another if they happen to come close together during the performance. This creates a false set of motion data which cannot be used without correction or reshooting.

Personal Magnetism

By far the most widespread motion-capture system in use today is that produced by Ascension Technology Co. of Burlington, Vt. Their system is magnetically based and requires the performer to wear a series of magnetic sensors, called birds, attached to the body points they want to track. Once these sensors are attached, the actor then moves around inside the strong magnetic field created by a large floor-mounted magnet.

As the performer moves, the system senses both the position and the orientation of each attached bird. Having both types of data available allows much more subtle motions, such as the turning of a wrist or waving of a hand, to be successfully captured.

The current difficulties with these types of motion capture systems are that they work in a much more limited area than an optical tracker, and they require the performer to wear a bulky suit of cables to connect each sensor to the computer. While it is not heavy, this wire harness does limit the range of movements.

Where's Waldo?

Waldos are everywhere in this field. A waldo is any mechanical control device that imitates the movements of the object it is controlling. They come in all shapes and sizes. There are waldo headsets that can be worn to track face, eye, and lip movements. There are waldo body suits to capture full-body motions. And there are waldo peripherals that look like joy sticks or puppet controls. These waldos are manually operated and can be used to animate any feature, such as eyes and ears, or fingers and toes, depending upon what parts of the computer object their motion is attached to.

Will Real Actors Be Replaced?

As synthetic actors and performance animation become ever more sophisticated, it is not hard to imagine one day watching synthetic actors performing alongside real ones. In fact, that has already happened on a relatively primitive level. It is extremely unlikely, however, that real actors will be replaced entirely, because they bring a level of talent and creativity that a synthetic actor can't begin to match. As with all of the other advances brought by digital technology, synthetic actors and performance animation will simply become another very useful tool in the service of visual storytelling.

With their motions captured from real actors, the Blockheads go for a spin in the MTV Liquid Television hit of the same name. Rather than replacing real actors, we are likely to see a growing collaboration between digital and real talent.

The Door Between Two Worlds: Embedding 3-D in Live Action

The gulf between the living and animated worlds is deep and wide and difficult to cross. Everyday reality is extremely rich and complex. Objects as common as trees, grass, and snowflakes have infinite variety; light and color mix and blend in countless subtle variations; and everything moves and responds quite naturally to everything else.

The world of computer graphics, on the other hand, is a poor shadow of this reality. Its elements all seem so solitary and self-contained that they couldn't interact unless forced to do so. The lighting is labored, the color blending and variation limited, and the natural objects so stiff and so far from nature that no one could possibly mistake them for something real.

As the silvery T1000 from the film *Terminator 2* leaves the scene of the crash, orange flames reflect from his legs and torso, while cool, sky-blue highlights are seen on his shoulders.

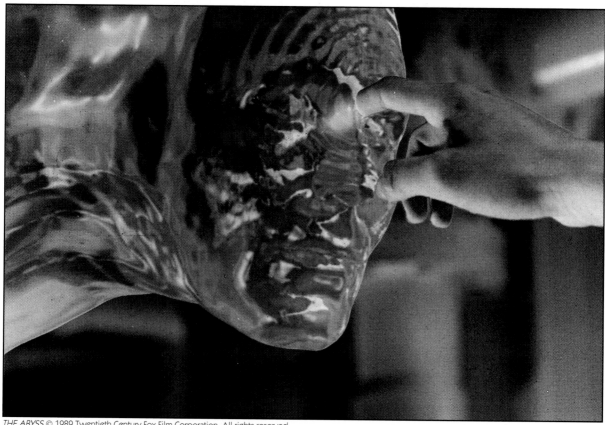

This image from the 1989 film *The Abyss*, was the first thoroughly believable interaction between a human and a computer graphic object. To make it convincing, the animators at Industrial Light & Magic made the watery face blink and ripple when the head was touched.

With these glaring differences between the two worlds, it is remarkable that they ever met. And yet they have, and they are continuing to do so with increasing regularity. How is it, then, that such widely separated worlds can interact so believably? The response from the people who produce these effects is generally a chuckle and the slightly guilty admission that "We cheat like mad. . . ."

This statement gets right to the heart of both the film and video production process. Whichever the medium, the goal is first and foremost to tell a story. Any visual trick that helps to convince the viewer of that story's reality can and should be used. In combining live action and computer graphics imagery, these visual tricks, or cheats, include shadowing, lighting, reflec-

Gilda, the sexy spoke-ant for VW-France is being interviewed by Henri Chapier for French public access TV. Although she is 100% computer generated, everything else is live action.

tion mapping, motion blur, and more. Each one serves to anchor the computer element inside the reality of the live action and convince both the eye and the mind of the audience that what they are seeing is actually happening.

Anchors Aweigh!

In any production requiring a mix of live-action and effects shots, it is up to the director to decide how best to capture each. For the effects, he or she must consider questions of cost, production time, and effectiveness before committing to a specific course of action. With the growing capability of computer graphics to create virtually any effect a director can imagine, it is easy to think that all effects should be done in computer graphics.

Here the live action is embedded in a computer graphics setting by mapping video images of the actor's faces onto the Blockheads' chunky computer bodies. Blockheads from MTV's Liquid Television.

While this may be theoretically possible, there are still many traditional special effects that can deliver the needed imagery in less time for less money. In addition, the problems of incorporating these more traditional approaches into live action are generally well understood. For example, animatronic robots are easily filmed as part of

To capture the lighting information on the live-action set of Fresca "Chuckling Straws," Pixar art director Andrew Schmidt placed a highly reflective steel ball in the middle of the table and photographed it. From the highlights on the ball, he was later able to reconstruct the lighting configuration.

© Pixar 1993

the live action itself, and miniatures can be lighted and shot in almost the same way.

All of the real-world approaches provide an immense amount of immediate feedback. The director can physically light, move, or touch the effects themselves, and the actors can interact with them directly. This sense of realism and immediacy is not available when working with computer-generated effects. The director instead must have faith, not only that the computer-generated elements will be properly modeled, but that they will also somehow fit inside the environment created on the live-action stage. It is not always an easy decision to make when considering computer graphics for an effects shot.

Get What You Need

Once the decision has been made to use computer graphics, the embedding process begins at once. Each live-action shot containing computer imagery must be planned with the graphics in mind. There is valuable information that has to be gathered at the time of shooting if the marriage between the live action and the computer imagery is to work.

Embedding computer graphics in live action means placing the computer image inside the live action shot so that they look as if they were filmed together.

Depending on the type of graphic to be embedded, the animators may need to know everything from the size and scale of the live-action set, to the lighting used, the distance the element is from the camera, the camera lens focal length, and the look of the surrounding set. The actual needs vary from shot to shot, but the general rule of thumb is always to get more than you think you need.

By Hook . . .

There are several ways to extract this information, some of which are manual and some automatic. The most common method is simply to measure the set directly by hand. After each live-action shot, a team from the animation department measures the size and placement of virtually every prop on the set. From this, they construct a computer model of the environment in which the 3-D graphic can move. Without such a mockup, it would be

Pixar/Colossal Pictures, 1992.

At one point in the French VW ad, Gilda the VW spoke-ant leans forward and flirts with the interviewer. His befuddled image, along with one of the stage lights can be seen reflected in her oversized computer-generated eyes.

As the soldiers march across the floor, the shadows follow in lock step. Without shadows, a computer graphic object has no substance in the real world.

Courtesy of Perrier Export.

very difficult to create a realistic motion path for it through the set.

The exactness of the measurement required depends on the amount of contact the computer-generated object has with any physical prop. For example, in Pixar's Fresca advertisement (See Chapter 12 "Fresca, Chuckling Straws") the measurements of the straws, the glasses, and their distances from each other and from the camera had to be very precise because the computer straws needed to look as if they were moving right against the rims of the glasses. For effects such as the pseudopod in *The Abyss*, however, measurements can be less exacting. There, the computer graphic element simply had to float through the middle of a fairly large volume.

. . . Or By Computer

Extracting all the needed data by hand is often prone to error because there is usually very little time to get it all down on paper. Live action for feature films can cost upwards of $100,000 a day, requiring the director to be as efficient as possible. This means that once a shot is finished, the set is either readied immediately for the following shot, or broken down so the next set can be built. So, any measurements not taken quickly become unavailable.

The ideal solution to the problem would be to use the computer to extract the 3-D data automatically from the film itself. For a long time, this was considered impossible. There is simply not enough information in any single 2-D film frame to recreate a three-dimensional set. Recently, this has changed. Solutions have been developed that analyze how elements in a scene change over

time. From these changes, the 3-D environment can then be inferred.

Some of these approaches require placing a reference object at a specific point in the set. Others, such as the one developed by Richard Chuang, co-founder of PDI, simply use elements in the shot itself. For example, when PDI was asked to put a dense fog bank over the mouth of New York harbor in Al Pacino's 1993 film, *Carlito's Way*, they scanned the series of frames into the computer. They then chose a set of known landmarks in the scene and watched how these varied as the film progressed. From this variation, plus a minimal amount of actual feature measurement, the computer produced a 3-D environment within which they created the fog bank.

Shadow, Light, Reflection

Knowing the sizes and spatial relationships of objects on a set is a good beginning. With this information, it is possible to create computer graphics objects that move realistically without bumping into props or actors. In addition, the computer can vary their apparent sizes as they move from foreground to background in order to maintain the proper perspective.

While all of this goes a long way toward convincing an audience that the object belongs to the real world, it is still not enough. Everything in reality interacts in some way with everything else. At the very least, objects cast shadows on each other, share the same lighting in identical environments, and reflect the colors and appearance of the world around them. If any one of these aspects is missing, the connection between the two worlds starts to

Courtesy of Carolco © 1991.

As the silvery T1000 from the film *Terminator 2* leaves the scene of the crash, orange flames reflect from his legs and torso, while cool, sky-blue highlights are seen on his shoulders.

break down. While the audience may not be able to say precisely what is wrong, they notice the difference and lose the ability to suspend their disbelief.

For example, without their shadows racing beside them, the stampeding gallimimus herd in *Jurassic Park* would have looked like ancient ghosts sailing above the grass. Without the eerie, blue light streaming from its watery body and falling on the walls as it passed, the entry of the creature into the underwater research lab in *The Abyss* would have seemed like a transparent overlay. And without detailed reflections of the surrounding world swirling over its metal skin, the T1000 in *Terminator 2* would have lost its convincing presence.

Creating Shady Characters

Since the behavior of light within the computer-generated world is completely under the animator's control, creating shadows is a relatively easy process. In fact, shadows are far easier to control in the computer world than on the live action set, where they are the bane of every director. In the real world, every light casts a shadow whether it is wanted or not, and the live-action lighting designer must go to great pains to be sure that none of them hides anything important.

On the computer set, however, lights operate differently. They don't cast shadows unless told to do so. Thus, multiple lights may be shined directly on a computer model, and only those lights that animators tell to will cast shadows. Lighting control, however, runs even deeper than this. Not only can animators specify the lights that will cast shadows, but they can also indicate which objects under those lights will or will not have shadows.

When creating shadows for use in a live action scene, the process is slightly more complex than simply turning on a computer light. The shadows must somehow fit the live-action environment into which they will be composited. It is important that the computer environment onto which the computer-generated shadows will be cast be as similar as possible to the live action set. Where the shadow would bend or shrink in the real world, it must do the same in the computer world.

This is because at the time the shadow is composited into the film frames, the live action is only a 2-dimensional picture. There is no 3-D environment to make the computer shadow behave any differently than it did on the computer-generated set. Once the shadow has been properly created, it is then extracted from the computer and pasted on the proper location in each film frame of the sequence.

Sharing the Limelight

For a computer graphics effect to be believable, the audience must be convinced that everything they see is happening in the same setting. This means all elements in every scene should look as if they have been lit by the same light sources. Nothing makes a computer-generated model stand out more from its live-action sequence than improper lighting. It acts like a signal flare and draws attention to itself just at the time the element should be blending in to its surroundings.

Creating the correct computer lighting means, once again, matching exactly what was used on the live-action set. This includes not only the number of lights, but their strength, colors, direction, and placement. This information is usually logged by hand during each shot and is often supplemented by placing a reflective metal ball in the set itself and photographing it. From the positions of the highlights on the ball's polished surface, computer animators can reconstruct an accurate lighting configuration.

> Compositing is the process by which the various elements in a given scene, such as blue screen shots, computer graphic objects, and live action, are combined to make a single image.

Once the basic lighting configuration is in place, color filters may be added to each light to match those used on the set. In the case of the Pseudopod in *The Abyss*, the live action was shot by moving a blue light along the corridors of the underwater lab. This created the feeling that something was passing through these areas. When the computer element was created, this same color light was used. So, when the creature was composited into the live-action sequence, it looked as if it were the source of the moving blue light.

If, however, the lighting configuration and colors still don't match the live setting, then the "cheating" begins. Cheating can include adding other lights, different colored gels, or selectively chosen shadows. As was mentioned in the section on lighting in Chapter 3, "The Process," computer light sources are invisible and can be placed anywhere they are needed without obscuring the image. These shadows, colors, and extra lights can help fine tune the object's appearance so it more closely matches what it should look like in the live action.

Take a Moment to Reflect

Look closely at the world that surrounds you. Smooth or polished surfaces glint and gleam, reflecting the light that has bounced off countless other nearby objects. This is the natural by-product of the physics of light. It gives our environment a richness and subtlety that only the most accomplished of artists can adequately convey.

Creating a Reflection

To create a reflection map, an animator first builds a 3-dimensional, rectangular shape inside the computer. On the inside of it, they then attach photos of the surrounding live-action environment to each wall of the rectangle. It's a bit like wallpapering a room, only in this case the wallpaper is a series of photographs that are stuck on the floor and ceiling, too. This "wallpapered" rectangle is then placed around the computer graphic object.

Once the rectangle is set, the computer then uses the photographs on the inside walls, ceiling, and floor, and reflects those images onto the surfaces of the computer-generated element. The end result is a computer effect, such as the water creature in *The Abyss* or the T1000 in *Terminator 2*, that appears to reflect its surroundings even though it was entirely created on the computer.

Because it is so ever-present, we notice its absence immediately. If something has a reflective skin, and yet it doesn't reflect its surroundings, then we know that it doesn't belong. Reflections, however, in computer graphics are very time-consuming to calculate. They require following and recording the interactions of millions of light rays as they pass through the environment.

The difficulty when producing a special effect to be combined with live action is that the entire environment is rarely available. This would mean building the full set, down to its finest detail, inside the computer. A colossal waste of time and money when all that is needed is the object itself. To overcome this problem, reflection maps that mirror the surrounding environment are used.

This process greatly heightened the reality of the scene in *Terminator 2* in which the T1000 smashes the police helicopter window and then flows inside. During the time it is reforming into the actor Robert Patrick, its silvery skin reflects the distorted and astonished face of the pilot.

The same thing was done to create the reflections glinting off the water-creature's skin in *The Abyss*. The technique is also widely used in the commercial graphics field, particularly in automobile advertisements where shiny reflective surfaces are used to sell the car.

There it Went! Adding Zip to Computer Images

Computer animations are created frame-by-frame. They are not produced by photographing a series of computer-generated elements moving around inside the computer. Given the speed with which a computer object or the computer camera is moving, each frame is calculated as a separate picture of the computer graphics environment at that moment. This creates a series of still pictures which when run together form the full animation.

Unfortunately, in real life, objects that move quickly past a camera with its shutter open produce a blurred image. This blur helps to promote the feeling of rapid motion, and also disguises short-comings in the projection technologies used for both film and television. These short-comings can be very noticeable when certain kinds of special effects, such as stop motion and computer graphics animation, are used.

Stop motion, which was used to produce the movements of the likes of King Kong and Godzilla, involves shooting film one frame at a time. In between frames, the model of the animal is moved to its next position. The result is a series of pictures of stopped motions.

Unfortunately, when run together for a film, this never looks quite real. There is a jittery quality to the movements that make them seem jerky. This jerkiness is an artifact of the double imaging used to project it. When something moves across the screen, the eye tracks the movement and creates expectations of where it should be at any time. Since each frame is shown twice, the actual motion on the screen doesn't match what the eye expects. The second exposure of each frame reveals the moving object still to be sitting at the same spot. This mismatch

The fearless T1000 has just leapt onto a flying helicopter and broken the windshield with a butt of his head. Through the break in the glass flows his liquid metal form. Look carefully at his skin to see distorted reflections of the entire cockpit.

makes the image appear to jump back and forth slightly, instead of moving smoothly across the screen.

You Mean I'm Seeing Double?

At the time Edison invented the motion picture camera and projector, he knew that the human eye needed to see a minimum of 48 frames per second. With anything below this rate, the eye began to notice the flicker caused by the darkness between the frames. This rate, however, was far too fast for the technology of the time to handle.

Fortunately, he discovered that film could be shot and projected at half that rate if, when it was projected, each frame was shown twice in a row. This same approach is still what is used today. For any projected film, the eye sees 48 frames each second, but only half of them are new.

It was discovered in computer graphics that if the edges of a moving object were blurred slightly this jittering effect could be smoothed out. The amount of blur to be added depends upon how fast the object is moving past the computer camera lens. The faster the object, the more spread out the blur. Unfortunately, this is a very expensive computer operation because instead of calculating a single point of the object per pixel, that point is often spread out over several pixels.

A pixel is the smallest unit into which the computer divides an image on the computer screen.

No End in Sight

Computer graphic effects are getting ever more complex and realistic. They are becoming more real not only because of the evolution in computer modeling and animation, but also because of a growing understanding of how to embed in live-action reality. Although it is still somewhat problematic for directors to work with computer effects, an increasing number of filmmakers are becoming comfortable with the technology, to the point where soon digital effects will be seen as one of the regular tools of the trade. With this increased acceptance, filmgoers can expect to see digital effects move ever more strongly out of the science fiction world and into standard dramas and other productions as well.

Getting It All Together: Compositing the Elements in Place

The theater is dark, the film rolls, and the fantasy begins. For the next two hours, a strip of celluloid images flashing on a silver screen will carry the audience to another world. If it has been properly produced, everyone watching will think and feel that what they are seeing is actually happening as they are seeing it.

This illusion of reality is of primary importance if any film or video is to succeed. The audience must be taken in or the story won't work. No one must guess that the full, rich image projected upon the screen is actually constructed from an extensive group of individually created elements. All evidence of the craft of filmmaking, such as wires and safety harnesses, blue or green screen photography, or defects in the film or lenses through which it was shot, must be hidden from sight. All the separately photographed elements must be gracefully melded together into one seamless image.

To create the bicyclists in this Perrier Advertisement, Industrial Light & Magic used rod puppets. The puppets have steel rods attached to their movable parts so they can be manipulated by a puppeteer. The rods were later painted out with a digital paint system.

This melding process, called compositing, is the last step before the film is edited into its final form. It is here that all the disparate film segments are united. As with virtually all the other steps of film or videomaking, this process, too, is being transformed by digital technology. Using the high-resolution scanners, powerful graphics computers, and film-printing technologies mentioned earlier, the art of making a film is becoming a science.

This does not mean that powerful visual stories are now the product of formula-driven computers. It means, rather, that the tools of filmmaking are becoming more precise and providing a level of visual control that was never before available.

The Way We Were

Film imagery, whether for television commercials or for feature productions, has always been created from collections of separate shots. The process of producing a film is far too complex to do otherwise. Each scene must be broken down into its most elementary form in order to ensure the maximum control over its execution.

Before digital image technology was available, all of the various shots for a given scene had to be composited together in a manually controlled optical process. A final image for any set of frames was built up through repeatedly exposing sections of those frames to light, using what are called mattes. Building a complex scene often required many different mattes to be cut along with multiple film exposures. The danger was that a single error at any stage could ruin the entire shot and force the optical crew to start from the beginning.

> A matte is a piece of opaque material that is laid across a film frame to block light from exposing the area of the film beneath it.

Place Tab 011010 into Slot 110010

With the introduction of digital technology, many of the earlier difficulties have disappeared, due to the fact that

Douglas Trumbull's simulator ride for the Luxor Las Vegas Hotel required the combining of live-action with both a computer-generated underground cavern, and a miniature model set filmed with motion-control cameras.

Courtesy of Mazda Motor of America

The Mazda MX-6 in the "Time Capsule" television commercial was first filmed on a live-action stage. Note the base on which the Mazda sits.

Here is the same image of the Mazda MX-6 with the computer-generated capsule, along with all its highlights and the surrounding setting composited into place.

Courtesy of Mazda Motor of America

everything in any film image, from its color to its brightness, is specified by an exact number. The process of compositing has become much more like assembling a well-labeled model. It is also considerably safer than the optical method and highly interactive. Whereas the optical process required lengthy, multiple exposures and film development time to see if the results were correct, digital compositing occurs on-screen as you watch. What's more,

there is no more exposure to the hazardous chemicals used in film development.

The optical film process also suffered from what is called generational loss, the same problem that afflicted early video technology. Essentially what generational loss means is that successive copies of any film frame are not identical to the frame from which it was created. This is because in nondigital duplication processes, some of the information that makes up the image is lost in the duplication process itself. If the pixels of an image are digital, however, then the number that represents any pixel is infinitely and exactly repeatable.

Singing the Blues

The most spectacular and visible digital special effects are the creation of 3-D objects, such as the dinosaurs in *Jurassic Park*. There is, however, a whole range of other digital visual effects whose quality is judged by what you don't see in the final film rather than by what you do. The use of blue screen photography is one such effect.

Blue screen photography is used to capture separate live-action elements that will later be composited into the primary film. These separate elements can be anything from actors, to models and miniatures, to natural features like trees or bushes. The process involves filming whatever the item is in front of a uniform, almost iridescent, blue backdrop. The blue of the screen is then eliminated from the picture, leaving only the element itself. This element can then be composited into various film sequences as desired, without bringing any other imagery along with it.

Courtesy of David Byrne.

For his digitally enhanced music video, "She's Mad," musician David Byrne could have just as easily been photographed against a green or red screen. Since Byrne wore flat black clothing for each shot, there was little concern for blue spill. See the "Oops, I Spilled the Blue" sidebar in this chapter.

Virtually every film and live-action television piece uses blue screen photography. The storm-tossed sailboat in *Captain Ron* was actually a model shot on a bobbing motion stand in front of a blue screen. Bruce Willis in *Death Becomes Her* inches across an insanely steep roof which looks like it is miles above the cobbled courtyard below. He was actually filmed against blue screen on a

(Photo by Drew Zelman) © 1993 The Trumbull Company. All Rights Reserved.

A live-action sequence from "In Search of the Obelisk," the Luxor Las Vegas Hotel's film-based simulator ride, is photographed against blue screen so that it can later be digitally composited with a miniature background.

model roof not more than four feet above the ground. And ace climber Sylvester Stallone in *Cliffhanger* looses his grip and drops his best friend's fiancée into a bottomless ravine. The film's dramatic opening was actually shot on a soundstage above a blue pad into which the flailing actress fell.

It's More Than Just the Blues

The choice of color is not nearly as strict as it used to be. In fact, green screen photography is now quite popular, and even red screen photography has been used. The intense blue of the blue screen was originally selected because of its unique optical properties. The chosen color rarely occurred in nature, and it could be eliminated from the image during the optical compositing process. Because of the requirements of the optical process, however, the blue of the screen had to be uniform throughout. If it weren't, then the fluctuations in color might prevent the optical process from eliminating all the blue and thus introduce unwanted visual effects in the final film frames.

Courtesy of Ketchum Advertising and Industrial Light & Magic.

This wild "Hot Wheels" ride in the 1994 Acura involved combining motion-control miniatures, live action, matte paintings, and computer effects. With current digital technology, imagination is truly the only limit to image making.

Oops, I Spilled the Blue

Blue spill is the term used to refer to the reflection of the colored backdrop on the surface of the item being filmed. The problem with it is that the blue highlights on the filmed item will be eliminated along with the blue of the background. The computer has no idea it is cutting away the desired object, it is simply selecting all pixels that contain the blue color. This can lead to rough edges that then require hand digital painting to correct. Blue, green, or red spill is the reason why highly reflective objects cannot be filmed using this process.

With the introduction of digital effects technology, however, automatic elimination of the blue screen has become a trivial problem. All that is required is for the effects technician to specify a range of values that corresponds to the color to be eliminated. The computer then examines the set of frames and cuts out every pixel that contains a color in that range.

This automatic color selection has also made it possible to experiment with other colors besides blue. Up until this point, no element photographed in this fashion could show any color similar to the blue of the screen. With the digital approach, however, it is now possible to switch the color of the screen and thus increase the range of colors available to the costume and set designers.

Cutting a Matte

The process of removing an element from one piece of film and placing it in another, often requires the creation of what is called a matte. Mattes are black and white pictures of the item to be composited. The white part is the part of the film you want to use, and the black part is what is to be left out.

For example, at one point in *Death Becomes Her*, actress Goldie Hawn has a hole shot through her middle by her rival Meryl Streep. Several times during the scene, the audience can see directly through the hole to what is behind her. The hole moved believably as Hawn moved.

To achieve this effect, a shot of the set without actors was first taken with a motion control camera. This created what is called the clean plate. Then Hawn and Streep were filmed with the same camera move as they circled each other. Hawn was wearing a shirt with a circle painted on over her stomach and her back. This circle was then used to create a matte which was applied to the clean plate. Wherever the matte shape fell on the clean plate, that section of the imagery was selected and transferred to the main film print. The result was a hole in her stomach through which the audience could see the rest of the set. For complete details of this scene, see Chapter 22, *"Death Becomes Her."*

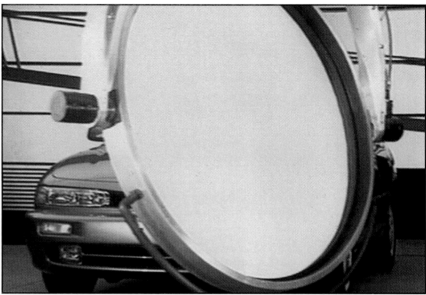

Courtesy of Grey Advertising and Rhythm & Hues.

A matte the size of the inner part of the loop has been created to remove that area of the picture. Once the inner image has been cut out, a new one can be laid inside.

Of Shamans and Shapeshifters

By now, virtually anyone who watches television or goes to the movies has seen the remarkable process of morphing. This is where one image transforms itself smoothly into another. Michael Jackson's "Black or White" music video used the technique to change one face into another in the longest morph sequence yet produced.

The technique of morphing was first experimented with back in the early 1970s at the New York Institute of Technology. It was not, however, until the late 1980s, with the release of the Lucasfilm movie, *Willow*, that it made its way to the public eye. During that film, a sorceress transforms from one creature to another before finally being revealed as herself.

Doug Smythe of George Lucas' Industrial Light and Magic effects house led the development of the morphing technique for that sequence. The software was not patented, but given to the public domain where it has since been used in countless television commercials, music videos, and films. For his efforts, the Academy of Motion Pictures gave Smythe a Technical Achievement Award in 1992.

Morphing Magic

Morphing is one of the few 2-dimensional digital effects. It is really an image-processing technique that takes two separate images, a starting point and an ending point, and transforms one into the other. With Smythe's

Photos of car transformation to tiger compliments of Exxon Company, USA, © Exxon Corp. 1994.

The morphing technique is sophisticated enough to take two totally unrelated images such as a car and a tiger, and smoothly transform one into the other.

method, both the starting and final images are covered with an identical grid of lines. Each intersection of the start grid is mapped to an intersection of the final grid.

For example, if you wanted to change a mouse into a lion, you would first place a grid over the mouse picture, being sure to cover only the mouse and not any of the surrounding imagery. You would do the same for the lion. Since the grids are the same, the squares in the grid would be much smaller for the mouse than for the lion. Once the intersections of one grid are connected to the intersections of the other, the process can begin.

The computer takes the two images, and, depending on how many seconds the morph is to take, transforms the shape of each image until they meet somewhere in the middle. The mouse is expanded until it is halfway to becoming a lion, and the lion is shrunk halfway to the mouse's size and shape. The computer also transforms the grey of the mouse and the yellow of the lion in the same way. The result is a smooth sequence of images that shows a gradual transformation of both. This sequence of changes is then composited into the live-action footage.

Lose the Wires!

With the advent of digital film technology, filmaking is getting sloppy. It is also getting a lot safer. It used to be that the intrusion of visible safety wires or any of the stuff of filmmaking, into the picture, would ruin a shot. Clearly from the audience's point of view, seeing a boom mike bobbing across the top of the frame wrecks that scene's believability.

With the advent of digital effects, however, this is no longer true. While it is always advisable to get as clean a shot as possible, mistakes can now be corrected "in digital." This also means that safety wires and harnesses can be much more substantial, making the process of stunt shooting safer. For example, in *Terminator 2*, Arnold Schwartzenegger, at one point, chases the T1000 by riding a motorcycle along the top of a cement wall bordering a drainage culvert. Suddenly, the wall ends, and he races the bike off the 15-foot edge. The motorcycle sails down behind the T1000, landing hard but upright, and the chase goes on.

The entire scene was shot with the motorcycle on a heavy beam with guy wires at either end attaching it to a primary safety cable. Clearly, the fearless terminator could not be shown in a truss of safety wires, so all of the cables and wires that lowered Schwartzenegger to the ground were erased from each of the frames.

Erasing wires, errors, and even whole groups of puppeteers needed for a special effect means that far less time needs to be spent on making sure a shot is clean. This means that directors can turn more of their energy to the art of storytelling, the heart of their craft.

Merging or Cloning Pixels

The manner in which wires and features are removed depends on how big they are. Thin wires such as those used to support actor Sylvester Stallone during the filming of the 1993 movie, *Cliffhanger*, can usually be erased automatically. The effects artist simply outlines the wire

To create the bicyclists in this Perrier advertisement, Industrial Light & Magic used rod puppets. The puppets have steel rods attached to their movable parts so they can be manipulated by a puppeteer. The rods were later painted out with a digital paint system.

Courtesy of Perrier Export.

The future has just begun. As startling and realistic as the digital dinosaurs were in *Jurassic Park*, they are only a hint of what is yet to come from the world of computer graphics.

for the computer, and the computer then takes the colors from pixels on either side of the wire and merges them together over the wire.

If the object is large, or the wire passes over a detailed background, however, merging won't work. In this case, each frame must be handled individually. Often it is possible to grab an area of the frame that looks the same as the hidden background, and paint it over the object to be eliminated. This is called cloning pixels, after the genetic duplicating technique developed in the field of biotechnology. If cloning doesn't work, then either a section of a clean plate—a shot of the empty set—can be used in the same way, or the effects person can simply paint out the element with a digital paint system.

Digital Crowd Duplication: Where Did All These People Come From?

When we talked earlier of digital actors eventually replacing real ones, the conclusion was that this would likely never happen. Human talent cannot be duplicated by the computer. This is not true, however, when it comes to crowd scenes. In fact, work for extras—actors that fill in the background of a shot—is shrinking in direct proportion to the advancement of digital film technologies.

It is now possible to take a small group of extras and simply duplicate them by computer to fill up the space. This

has saved films like *The Babe*, *In The Line of Fire*, and others, a large amount of money and headache. Fewer extras need to be paid, and the logistics of crowd management are greatly eased. For *The Babe*, Pacific Data Images (PDI) turned 1,000 extras into crowds of over 20,000 spectators. These duplicated extras were then fitted into various computer models of stadiums that existed during that era. In many scenes, individual extra actors appeared over 15 times, but with the random duplication and placement approach PDI developed, it was impossible to tell.

It's Only Just Beginning

Until recently, the process of filmmaking was almost entirely optical. Over the last few years this has changed dramatically. Digital technology has become the real workhorse of both the film and television industries, offering a level of dependability and control that was not previously possible.

In the future, it is likely that virtually all of the tasks of filmmaking will become digitally based. As the technology continues to get cheaper and performance better, it may be that film itself will eventually disapppear, spawning a whole new look for the visual arts. The most remarkable aspect of all of this is that, despite the massive inroads into the film and television industries that digital imagery has made to date, it has really only just begun.

Live and Up Close

Now it is time for a look at computer graphics in action. The following group of chapters takes individual productions from television spots to music videos to films, and examines what made the special effects work so well in each. The best and most exciting work created to date was used in order to show just how computer imagery is changing what we see and how we see it.

The world of computer graphics is expanding at an awesome rate, and this section is intended to provide both a look at where it has been recently, and at least a glimpse at where it is going in the future.

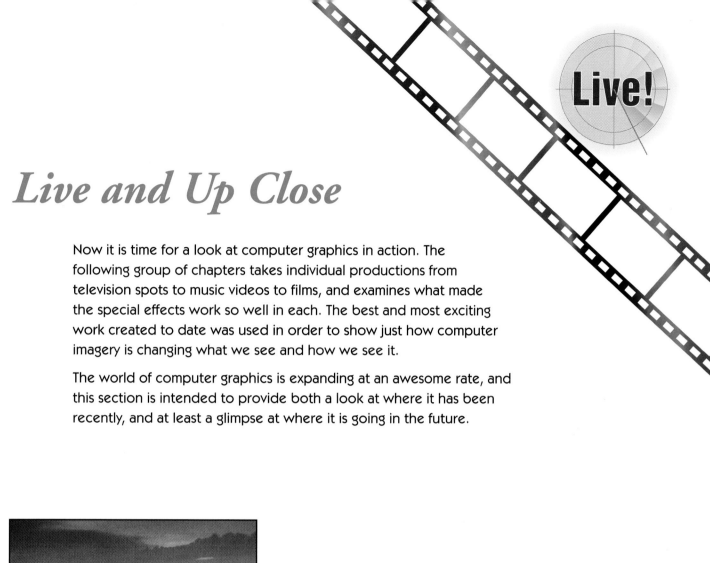

9

42,000 Frames Twice: The Incredible Crash Dummies

With a growing crescendo of rock music, the cartoon begins. Slick, standing at a taxi stop, hears a screeching of skidding tires. As the song begins, "Through thick and thin, Slick and Spin get the job done," the taxi crashes through the brick wall behind him. Slick hops in to join Spin, the driver, and off they careen together.

Heroes Slick and Spin get a briefing from Dr. Zub about an upcoming test.

Slick and Spin at the test track, preparing to crash-test their motorcycles.

"When there's no hope in sight, crash, crash dummies will make things right," continues the song. The taxi disappears over a rise in the road, quickly followed by a horrendous crash. Parts of the wreckage fly forward to form the words "The Incredible Crash Dummies," introducing the cartoon.

From 30 Seconds to 22 1/2 Minutes in a Single Bound

This screeching, crashing opening of "The Incredible Crash Dummies" starts the first full-length television cartoon created entirely in computer graphics. Created as a pilot for a possible upcoming show, it was completed in March of 1993, after six grueling months of intense effort by a team of twelve Minnesota-based animators. It marks a major milestone for the computer graphics industry as well as for Lamb & Company, the 20-person Minneapolis-based computer graphics company responsible for the piece. The fact that such a production was possible at all, and that it did not come from one of the major West or East Coast studios, says worlds about how far both computer graphics software and hardware have come.

Lamb & Company has been working in the computer graphics field for almost ten years now, and, like virtually all the other commercial computer graphics studios, has concentrated on flying logos, show openings, and television spots. The longest piece of work they had previously attempted was only 30 seconds in duration, so to make the step from that to a full half-hour cartoon was a monumental leap.

It Just Ain't the Same

While theaters used to provide space for multiminute cartoons before the main feature, this opportunity has largely disappeared. These days, computer animators have essentially three time slots to program for: the 30-second TV spot, the half-hour Saturday morning cartoon, and the 75–90-minute animated feature.

Thirty-second commercials are only 900 frames long. They may be quite complex and involve very sophisticated graphic effects, but there is only so much that can be done within that time period. With commercials, characters are usually shallow, the scene and shot changes are limited, and there are few worries when it comes to action continuity and sophisticated mood lighting.

Once computer animation moves to the half-hour cartoon, however, everything is different. Suddenly, a full story has to be told. Characters must be fully developed, and the whole production, from the action to the look and feel, must somehow hang together. This is by no means an easy process, particularly in a computer environment where every detail shown must be meticulously planned and executed.

Setting Up

When Larry Lamb, founder and executive producer of Lamb & Company, announced in September, 1992, that the studio had won the Tyco Toys contract for Crash Dummies, there was actually very little cheering. Even though the entire staff knew it was the opportunity of a lifetime, they also knew that they didn't really understand how to do it. They felt they had the expertise, but the immensity of the project was overwhelming.

Since they were the first to tackle such a piece, there was also no one to call for advice, no books to read, no consultants to hire, or anything to help them find their way. In addition, all their tools, the software and hardware with which they did their work, were set up to handle 30 seconds of animation at the most. Everything had to be changed if they were to succeed.

New Tools

The first eight weeks were almost entirely taken up with creating the sets and models for the show. For this, their Wavefront modeling software worked perfectly. As the modeling team began their work, Lamb's four software

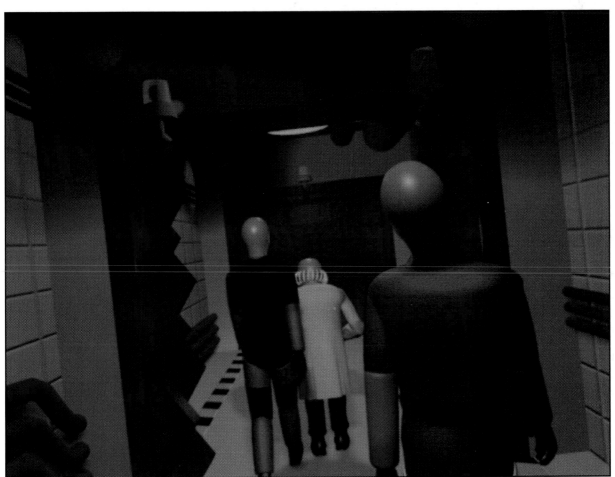

Slick and Spin entering the high-security section of the test track. Note the interesting camera tilt, plus shadows and highlights not easily created with standard animation.

© 1993, Tyco Industries.

Can computer graphics be funny? In a bit of slapstick, Ted calmly paints the Crash Dummy symbol as his test sled rockets around the track.

Controlling the Animation

The second major tool was a system to track and control the billions of bytes of information being generated. While a standard television commercial requires a maximum of three animation files to hold all the specifications for scenes, props, characters, lighting, and so on, the Crash Dummies cartoon ended up with over 200 such files.

engineers dug into the process of creating support tools. The first thing they did was write their own rendering program, called a renderer. The renderer is what takes modeling, lighting, and animation data and turns it into final images. They wrote their own program to give them greater control over the show's look and feel and to make better use of their network of twenty Silicon Graphics computers.

Their new system automatically sent frames needing to be rendered over the network to whichever machines were not busy. This was a key tool for getting the job done. A half-hour cartoon is 22 1/2 minutes of animation after the time for commercials is deducted, which translates to approximately 42,000 separate frames. With the number of test animations required per shot, it would have taken one of their machines about 2 1/2 years of steady number crunching to get it all done.

In order to keep this data from overwhelming the animators, the technical staff wrote a program that allowed the animators to assemble any given scene simply by calling for the required items. Thus, if an animator was working on the test track scene, he or she could just tell the computer what models were needed in which set, and the computer would bring them together. Without such a system, hundreds of files would have had to have been searched to find the right items.

The animation system also allowed the animators to focus strictly on the part of the action they were then animating. For example, if an animator was working on a scene in Junkman's castle, an extremely complex set full of Junkbots, Crash Dummies, Junkman himself, and his amazing brain-sucking machine, he or she could switch off everything but what was being worked on. Thus, if an

Are Computer Graphics Funny?

Before landing this job, Lamb & Company had previously completed a series of Crash Dummy advertisements. This gave them a head start when Tyco made the decision to bring out a Crash Dummy cartoon show. Tyco also looked at standard 2-dimensional animation, but realized they already had considerable equity in the computer look Lamb had created for them. However, since a full 3-D graphics cartoon show had never been done before, they questioned whether computer graphics could be funny.

From looking at the largely stiff and lifeless graphics of past years, it is possible to get this impression. In those days, the underlying technology greatly inhibited what could be expressed. Fortunately, Lamb was able to convince Tyco that the technology no longer presented the same problems, and that good humor flowed from good animation, whether the computer or a pencil was used to produce it.

arm movement was being specified, only that arm was shown on the computer screen. After the movement was completed, it could then be viewed in context with the other elements of the scene.

The Bottom Line

A half-hour show of standard 2-D animation can cost between $300,000 and $500,000. While the cost of computer animation has come down greatly, it is still quite a bit more than that. Lamb & Company's budget for the Crash Dummies was $700,000, which did not cover their own sizable investment in the new equipment and software needed to complete the project. Lamb estimates, however, that with the experience they gained and the new systems they have in place, that a second half-hour would be considerably cheaper.

Here a Light, There a Light

Lighting for many of Lamb & Company's television commercials is usually very straightforward. Everything is washed with a cheery, shadowless light that is bright enough to make the featured products stand out. Once an animation begins to tell a story, however, this changes radically.

Evoking a story's mood requires dramatic lighting that pools in some areas, casts shadows, and uses color. Unfortunately, every light added to a scene costs money. Because of this, most scenes in the Crash Dummies cartoon were limited to six lights. Larger sets like the giant test track required up to sixteen lights, but most scenes were able to stay within the prescribed number.

Regardless of the number of general lights per shot, however, only three of them were allowed to cast shadows. These three shadow casters were usually placed in the foreground to highlight the action. This allowed a great deal more control of the mood, and also served to fool the viewer's eye into thinking that all the lights in the scene cast some kind of shadow.

Most of the lights used throughout the show were standard white. It was not until the appearance of Junkman's cave, a massive, skull-shaped heap of junk, that color began to play a part. There, the lighting design team had to deal with heavy shadowing and colored lights to set the dark mood, and a bilious, green sky that could be seen through the doors and windows. Working with colored computer lights is particularly difficult when they are shined onto colored objects. The resulting hue is a combination of the two colors rather than the more intuitive expectation of the light's color appearing as highlights on the receiving object.

Through the Canyon

The scene which showed Slick and Spin approaching the cave through an orange canyon illustrates some of the problems. The idea was to evoke the sense that the two Dummy heroes were walking into a polluted and poisoned environment. The surrounding rocks of the canyon were a glowing orange, and cast dirty, orange

Slick, Spin, and the Doctor enter to find the lab in a shambles. To create this mess, the animators merely tipped the tables on their sides and the computer rendered the way they looked.

© 1993, Tyco Industries.

Junkman and his Junkbots in his cave. Green sky, orange rocks, and deeply shadowed mood lighting help evoke the Junkman's character. To animate complex scenes like this, any part of this image can be turned off to help the animator focus on the action.

© 1993, Tyco Industries.

shadows, while the clouds in the sky circled above them in dingy shades of green.

To create the orange canyon, the lighting team shined orange lights across the entire landscape and told the orange lights not to cast any shadows. The results were eerie and foreboding. The only problem was that when the heroes entered the canyon, they too became orange, and it made the whole scene look as if it were covered by a filmy gauze. To remedy this problem, they decided to light the Dummies in white light. At the same time, however, they wanted orange shadows to fall across them as they moved past the various rock formations.

Since they wanted shadows from the rocks, they couldn't simply attach white lights to the Dummies' bodies. This would have washed all other lighting effects away. The solution was to take a second light whose color, cyan, when mixed with orange produced white. That light was instructed to cast shadows from each of the rock outcroppings. This meant that when the Dummies passed a rock, the cyan light was blocked leaving only the orange. And when they emerged from the shadow, the cyan would combine with the orange to produce white.

A long view of the test track. This large interior space required 16 computer lights to illuminate it. Note shadows, lighting, and perspective, all of which are calculated automatically by the computer.

© 1993, Tyco Industries.

Guerrilla Filmmaking

When the project began, director Mark Mariutto and producer Pam Lehn figured they had to produce over half a minute of finished animation per day if they were to meet their deadline. In fact, there was a saying around the company at that time which went "A thousand frames a day, keeps the lawyers away." At the start, this much animation, day after day, looked like a prodigious quantity. By the time they finished the project six months later and a week ahead of schedule, they were working at a clip of over 5,400 frames a day.

When the work began, there was also considerable grumbling about how much there was to do, but as the project wore on, everyone rose to the occasion. Two months into it, virtually the entire staff was working at least 12 hours a day, seven days a week. The dedication was so high, that a rule prohibiting work after midnight had to be instituted. At that time, all the machines were then turned over to rendering the frames created that day so they would be ready for daily review the next morning.

One of the programming staff baby-sat the network of machines while they steadily crunched away on the images. If the process was going smoothly, each computer would give off the contented lowing of a cow in the fields. However, if something went wrong, the machine with the problem would sound like breaking glass. The staff member on hand would then try to repair either the image data or the rendering software, whichever was the source of the problem.

Shadowing

Shadow casting vastly increases the cost of any light because it requires the computer to look through the light and see what objects it notices. It should be remembered that in a computer set, lights see only the objects they have been told to see. Light may shine right through some things, but bounce off others depending on the effect the lighting designer wants.

For each object seen by the light, the computer then calculates a shadow. If the surface onto which the shadow falls is flat, the application of the shadow to that surface is fairly easy. But, if the shadow falls onto other objects like chairs, people, or irregular shapes, then the complexity of the problem, and thus the time to render it properly, increases significantly.

Junkman's cave, a jumble of skull-shaped wreckage set against an ominous grimy-green sky. The canyon below is washed with an orange computer light to give it a fiery glow.

© 1993, Tyco Industries.

Morning Reveille

Each morning began with dailies, a review of the shots completed the day before. Here, director Mariutto and producer Lehn would step through each scene and each frame pointing out what needed correction and what would pass. The highest highs came for the animators when they saw that their new material had turned out exactly as they had hoped. The lowest lows resulted when they saw that the frames they thought were perfect needed extensive revisions.

Each animator would then leave the dailies with a list of repairs to the previous day's work and the next shot to be tackled. Lehn would add the finished frames to the digital tape library and chart the overall progress.

Maintaining the Vision

Once the fixes for the previous day's animation were complete, new work could begin. While the intent at the start of the show was to assign characters to individual animators, the crush of production prohibited this. Whoever was available was simply put on the next shot to

be completed. While this is an efficient way to turn out completed frames, it does not necessarily produce the best quality animation because it is difficult to maintain character consistency.

Make Your Own Lights

One of the key elements to producing a rich 3-dimensional look is reflected highlights. For example, if a ball is held above a smooth surface and a light is shined from above, the bottom of the ball is lit by light reflected from the table below. True reflection in computer graphics, however, is very expensive, requiring a lot of number crunching. Fortunately, the truth is not what is needed; all that is required is the appearance of the truth. So, the Lamb lighting designers created a light which, when shined on one side of an object, spread a lesser amount of light on the other side.

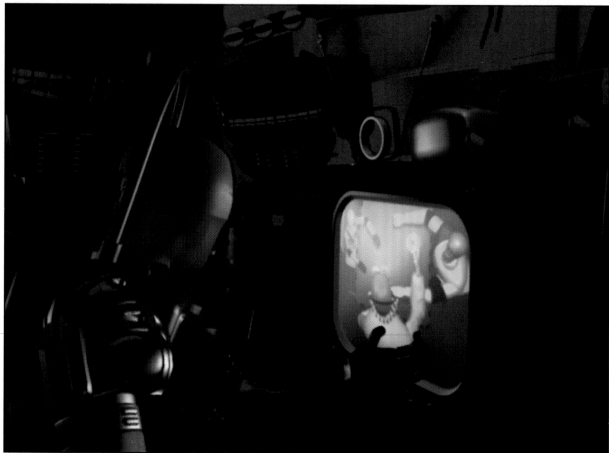

© 1993, Tyco Industries.

Junkman spying on the Crash Dummies from his lair. Note the scene's detail. Everything you see had to be built by hand. Also note the highlights on Junkman's head and shoulder that make it seem as if the TV light is glinting off of them. The toaster on top has a second highlight from these first two.

Dr. Zub is trapped. Using his ingenious brainsucker, Junkman means to get the secret plans for the Torso 9000.

Despite this difficulty, Mariutto's direction was able to forge a single vision among the animators. Little by little, with the wink of an eye, the twitch of an eyebrow, or the wiggle of a mustache, the Dummies came to life.

Free at Last

All told, "The Incredible Crash Dummies" required Lamb & Company to animate 66 separate scenes with over 300 different shots. It was estimated also that most of the frames had to be created at least twice, once for various tests and once for final rendering. This all translated to over two gigabytes (billions of bytes) of animation data by the time they finished, a prodigious amount by anybody's standards.

By the end of the project, they had worked almost their entire waking lives, both day and night, throughout the cold Minnesota winter. Finally, like a bear awakening from hibernation, they emerged in early spring to face the world with the first full-length computer-animated cartoon in hand. The cartoon was debuted on May 1, 1993 to great acclaim. With their success, the industry now knows it is possible, and it will certainly not be the last.

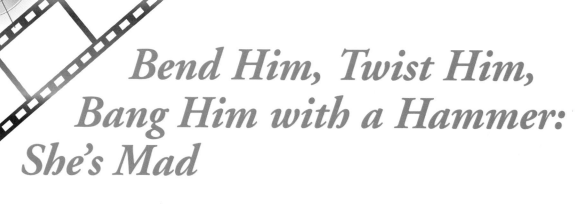

10

Bend Him, Twist Him, Bang Him with a Hammer: She's Mad

A driving, relentless pulse of rock and roll opens this music video. The lone figure of David Byrne appears standing in a large expanse of gray. The camera moves closer. "Banging his head . . ." the words begin, as a plate flies in from the upper left and smashes against his head. "Stab in the back . . ." Byrne's shocked face fills the camera. His reddened eyes open wider than humanly possible, and two black spirals swirl behind his pupils.

Rubber man David Byrne morphs to his music in "She's Mad." The video was nominated for two MTV music video awards that year: best special effects and best new concept.

Courtesy of David Byrne.

Courtesy of David Byrne.

Talk about loose! Byrne's arms snake up and down as if they have no bones.

The music pulls the imagery onward, each phrase of the song bashing, bending, and transforming Byrne's body until the final sequence where he breaks into a swarm of particles, somehow comes back together, and ends the song.

All in a Weekend's Fun

David Byrne's captivating music video, "She's Mad" came together in a single, grand crescendo of work and fun over an extended President's Day weekend in 1992. That was when over twenty programmers and animators from Pacific Data Images gathered in PDI's Los Angeles studios to create this immensely successful music video.

The story actually began a few weeks earlier when producer Lexi Godfrey came to Glenn Entis, founder and executive producer of PDI, with the idea of doing Byrne's next music video. Entis immediately liked the idea, and Byrne visited the studio with his storyboard in hand. Byrne's enthusiasm for what he saw led him to

redraw the storyboards to include the use of some 30 different computer-effects shots.

Can We Do It?

There was no doubt in the minds of either Entis or art director Carlos Arguellos that they wanted to do it and that it could be done. None of the effects required breaking new ground in the science of computer graphics. The difficulty lay in whether they could accomplish everything within the severe restrictions of a music video budget. A typical three- to four-minute music video costs around $100,000 to produce, while a 30-second computer graphic television commercial can be many times that amount. Clearly, this vast difference meant the company could not afford to interrupt their normal production schedule. If they were to take on the project, an alternative approach would have to be used.

Entis decided to open the whole thing up to the entire company to see what others thought. With a huge contingent of dedicated David Byrne fans in the company, the response was overwhelmingly positive. Everyone wanted to do it, even if it meant giving up a weekend to get it done. In the end, that is precisely what it did require, and the company asked for volunteers to work outside the normal production schedule.

The Work-Party

Over twenty animators and programmers jumped at the chance, including over a dozen from PDI's northern office in Sunnyvale, CA. The folks from out of town were flown in on the Friday evening of the long President's Day weekend, and the fun began. Each staff member had previously picked his or her favorite effect to work on and was ready to go when the work began on Saturday morning.

Throughout the weekend days, the animators chugged away on creating their morphs, 3-D elements, and other effects. At night, Byrne would visit the studio to check the progress and to direct the further work needed. Even though everyone worked amazingly hard, the enthusiasm

was so high that it seemed as if a weekend-long party was in session.

Of Hammer Heads, Spiral Eyes, and More

There were over 30 effects shot in the four-minute computer-graphics extravaganza of "She's Mad," involving morphs, 3-D elements, blue screen work, and more. Almost every line in the song was illustrated by an effect. Due to space constraints, all of them cannot be discussed in detail, but the following shots represent a substantial cross section of the work done.

Hammer Head

" . . . and turn around and hit him with a hammer." Another punishing line in the song, and a carbon steel hammer as big as a man's body descends from the left and smashes onto the top of Byrne's head. The upper part of his skull squishes out in either direction, while the

Courtesy of David Byrne.

A king-sized headache: The giant hammer descends, and his head bulges. Yet David Byrne sings on.

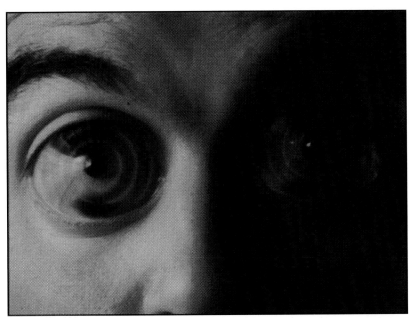

Courtesy of David Byrne.

Red spirals in superwide eyes mark the performer's surprise. The pupils were morphed smaller to show more of the spirals, and the highlights and glints were laid on top after the spirals were inserted.

whole head jams down onto his shoulders. His face is contorted into a painful grimace as a hairless bump rises at the point of contact. Fortunately for Byrne, it's only his image that takes the hit.

The Hammer Head sequence, as it is called, looks deceptively simple, but, in fact, involved the assembly of several different elements, and the application of the image warping technique of morphing. The effect began with a blue screen shot of Byrne standing, holding his guitar and singing the deadly line. As he sang, a hand holding a large square of opaque board came into the frame from the right. The hand brought the board sharply down towards his head without actually landing a blow.

Shadows and Timing

This provided Byrne with the timing for his grimace, and also introduced a shadow that art director Arguellos thought would anchor the hammer in reality. The theory was right, but in shooting the next element, the hammer, they made an error that animator Karen Schneider would later have to correct. The hammer was filmed in a close-up against blue screen to make it seem very large, but it was shot coming down from the left instead of the right.

This meant that the shadow introduced by the previous shot with the opaque board was on the wrong side of Byrne's head. Schneider remedied the situation by using the computer to flip the shadowed element of Byrne so that when the hammer came down, the shadow would be in the correct position.

This was not all she changed, however, because she also felt the hammer moved far too slowly to impart the necessary drama. Schneider was able to speed up some sections by dropping selected frames from the shot.

Morphing and Compositing

After the hammer element and the Byrne element had been extracted from their blue screen shots, they were overlaid to test the action. Schneider positioned the hammer to hit square in the center of Byrne's head and then designed the head morph around it. She set the morphing control lines so the head would appear to squish down and out, much like a blob of Silly Putty; the computer did the rest, distorting Byrne's head as commanded. The results were then composited into the background plate.

At this point, for all intents and purposes, the effect was complete. However, Schneider was not happy with the final look. It didn't seem to provide the humor she thought it should have. To remedy the situation, she added a bump rising from the middle of Byrne's head as the hammer pulled away. It looked like a bald egg, just like something from the cartoon world, and Byrne loved it. All it took was a little extra morph to warp the center of his head upwards, and then a patch of skin copied from a part of Byrne's forehead. Once the skin patch was laid over the bump, it looked perfect, and the effect was truly complete.

Spiral Eyes

"Bangin' his head. Stab in the back. . . ." The harsh lyrics begin. As his back gets stabbed, Byrne's reddened eyes expand to fill much of the screen. Black spirals rotate wildly behind his pupils, drawing you into his pain, creating another few-second effect that is far more than it appears. This one did not need any blue screen work, but it did require animator Ken Bielenberg to build the spirals as a 3-D computer graphics element.

Although it appears that the effect could have been created by simply mapping 2-D spirals directly onto Byrne's eyes, Bielenberg wanted an image that would really draw the viewer in. For this, he needed to be able to show the spirals actually receding into the eyeballs themselves.

Wide Eyed

The modeling itself was relatively simple, and Bielenberg was able to build it quickly. Once the spirals were complete, he then had to figure out how to embed them in the eyeballs. The first step was opening the eyes really wide.

PDI's in-house image-morphing tool was used here. Morphing usually takes one image and transforms it smoothly into a second different image. In this case, however, the tool was used simply to distort a single picture. After a few attempts, the desired eye-stretch was produced, not only expanding the width of Byrne's eyeballs, but contracting his pupils so the spirals would show more clearly.

Courtesy of David Byrne.

Singer/Songwriter David Byrne shown on a turntable playing his guitar. He was shot against blue screen and was pulled out from the background to create the rotating exorcist effect.

Digital Eye Surgery: Implanting the Spirals

Once the eye size was set, it was time to open them up and insert the spirals. The idea was to fix the rotational center of the spiral right behind the pupils. Bielenberg knew that for the effect to be believable, the spirals had to stay locked to their appropriate spots in the picture. If they jittered or swam about inside the eyes, the effect would be ruined.

To extract the necessary placement data, he used one of PDI's image tracking tools. With the resulting information that described precisely how Byrne's eyes moved, Bielenberg was then able to anchor the spirals to the backs of the pupils. Before he inserted them, however, he first blurred the 3-D images slightly to hide their computer-generated origin. Computer images can have a hard-edged smoothness that makes them stand out when they are composited into film. Blurring them or adding digital film grain eliminates this problem.

Courtesy of David Byrne.

In the midst of his time displacement spin, various sections of Byrne's body appear to turn at different rates, creating a corkscrew effect.

Finishing Touches

At this point, it was time to decide on the eye color and to add highlights to make the whole effect more convincing. Bielenberg first tried a shade of yellow, which Byrne quickly nixed. Byrne was looking for a more crazed look, and so together they settled on red. They also decided how fast the spirals should be made to spin.

After this, Bielenberg then went back to the original footage and cut out Byrne's pupils and a series of highlights on the surface of his eyes. He then laid these highlights, glints from the live-action lights, over the morphed and spiraling eyes, and the effect was finished.

Courtesy of David Byrne.

Beyond the splits. Byrne plays his guitar as his legs perform on their own.

Rotating Exorcist

"I know! I say! I'm findin' out today. Some way! Somehow! I'm gonna pull you down." Singing of destruction, Byrne stands impassive before the viewer. Slowly, he begins to rotate. His head turns, but his body from the neck down turns more slowly. In fact, as the image proceeds, his entire body gradually twists into a revolving corkscrew which has become known as the rotating exorcist.

Though this effect appears to be one of the more complex visuals of the video, it actually was one of the most straight-forward. It grew directly out of Shawn Neely's research into image manipulation. Neely, normally part of PDI's research team, had developed what he calls a time displacement system that allows him to build an image out of parts clipped from other frames in a given sequence.

Scanning the Past

To create the effect, Byrne was first shot in live action spinning slowly on a turntable before a blue screen. Neely then extracted Byrne's image for this group of frames and set his program to work on it. He instructed the program to take different lines of the image (scan lines) from the various frames in the sequence. In order to make a smooth spiral, each scan line below the midpoint in Byrne's neck was taken from one of the previous frames. For example, if the line being created was two lines down from the neck point, it was plucked from the frame located two frames back in the sequence. If it were

three lines down, then it would be taken from three frames back, and so on, until an entire image was built.

> Aliasing in computer graphics often appears as a jagged-looking line in computer-generated or altered images.

Although the process was largely automatic once it started, it was not problem-free. Neely had to deal with an aliasing effect that made the transition from one image line to another somewhat jagged. To remedy the situation, he tried blurring the borders between the lines by combining each line with small bits of the lines immediately above and below it. Although the ideal solution would have been to film Byrne's turntable sequence with high-speed cameras, this merging approach did the trick and completed the "rotating exorcist."

Wavy Gravy

" . . . Look where you're goin'. You don't even know what you're knowin'. . . ." Byrne sings the easy, almost island, rhythm of the chorus as his legs bend and wave and stretch far beyond what is humanly possible. As the chorus continues, Byrne appears totally unconcerned with the contortions of his limbs, as if they belonged to somebody else.

To create the effect, art director Arguellos' live-action team began by filming Byrne against a blue screen. At first, they thought that he ought to move his own arms and legs as close to the distorted motions as possible. This, however, turned out to be more trouble than it was worth, because with the greater movements, it became harder for animator Roger Gould to match the morph to the live action. In the end, they decided to refilm. Byrne was allowed to do whatever he liked with his hands and his head, but his limbs had to stay as still as he could manage.

From this footage, Gould extracted Byrne and began the morph, wobbling his legs, waving his arms, and stretching the limbs beyond normal human endurance. Once the morphs were finished and approved, they were then composited into the background plate to produce one of the funnier scenes in the video.

Particle Man

As if being stretched and distorted by Gould's morphs weren't enough, Byrne's already tortured body next suddenly explodes into a million glowing particles. These bright, firefly-like specs swarm around each other, moving from chaos to a vaguely discernible shape that gradually coalesces back into Byrne's guitar-playing form as the video draws to a close.

Going to Pieces

The effect required using two very interesting pieces of technology. The first was a performance animation suit, and the second was PDI's particle system software. Particle software generates numbers of small visible elements, as many as an animator wants. Each of these particles can then be told how to behave, and they each behave independently of any other particle. Their behaviors include not only how they move, but how their sizes change over time, and what colors they will exhibit.

In this case, animator Graham Walters used a selection of colors and sizes, along with one basic behavior. Each of the particles used what was called the "moth and flame"

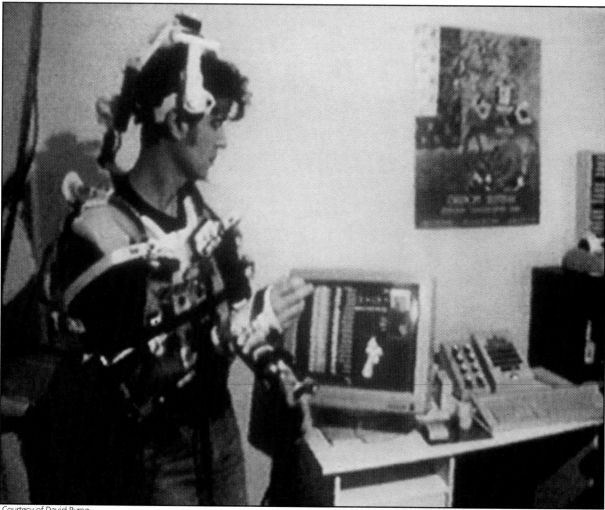

Courtesy of David Byrne.

David Byrne shown wearing the PDI exoskeleton used to capture his movements for the particle man sequence.

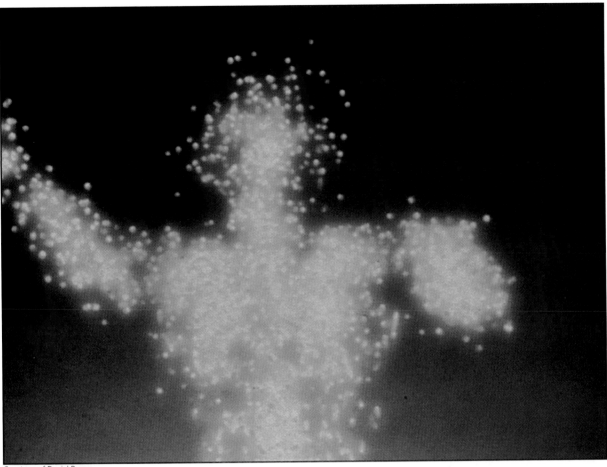

Courtesy of David Byrne.

Brilliant, self-lit particles cluster where the performer's body used to be.

procedure to guide their movements. With this program, Walters specified a target flame, in this case elements of Byrne's body, and the particles then swarmed around them. In addition, the colors and sizes of the particles varied as the sequence progressed.

At first, the dots were very small and very bright white. Gradually, the number of particles decreased while the size of the remaining ones grew. As the size grew, their colors changed, too. They began to take on the colors from the nearest spot on Byrne's body. Slowly, the swirling masses of dots began to look like a ghostly image of Byrne himself, until at last, the particles merged completely to reveal the singer.

Grabbing the Motion

During this time, Byrne is also singing and dancing, and the swarms of particles are somehow following his movements. As his arm moves, the system of dots swirling around it moves, too. The movements are distinctly the

singer's own, and there is no sense of discontinuity when the actual image of Byrne reassembles itself at the end of the sequence.

The transition is smooth because all of the motion used to create the particle man was taken directly from Byrne himself. To create the movements, he donned PDI's motion-capture suit, an exoskeleton of metal, wires, and potentiometers that measured in real time the angles of his various joints. As he danced, the computer translated the captured data into 3-dimensional positions that could be applied to move a 3-D computer model.

During the motion capture, Byrne was able to watch a low-resolution image of a 3-D figure dancing on a computer screen as he himself was dancing. Once Byrne was satisfied with the motion, Walters then connected it to the 3-D volume around which the particles were to swarm, providing an eerie feeling of solidity, and a stunning ending to this fun-packed piece.

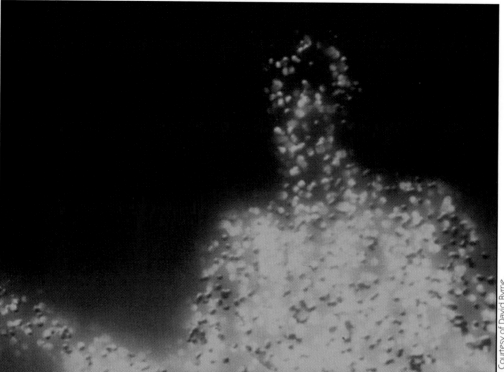

The particles have grown larger and their colors stronger as the singer slowly takes back his human form.

Courtesy of David Byrne.

Other Wonders

Other effects included turning Byrne into a singing house, creating a neighborhood of these houses, stretching his ear, morphing him into a series of animals, and turning his face into mud, to name but a few. To turn out such a quantity of computer graphics work in such a short time says a lot for both the people involved and the amount of progress that has taken place in the field of computer graphics. Except for one or two of the more difficult spots, each of the 30 visual effects was started and completed over a single work-party weekend, and each made a substantial contribution to one of the most humorous and eye-catching music videos yet made.

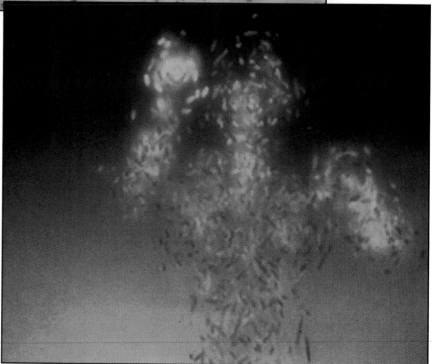

Courtesy of David Byrne.

Losing their inner glow, the particles start to take on colors from Byrne's own image.

Blowing Away the Old: The Lexus ES 300

This 30-second television commercial opens with a shot of a car in the middle of a grassy field. The car is covered by a white, parachute-like piece of material. As the voice-over begins, a breeze starts to ripple the white car cover.

While the first image might be mistaken for a morph, there is no doubt that the older model has become a skin that the new Lexus is shedding. Since Rhythm & Hues did not use a morphing approach, they were able to bend and twist the skin in a very realistic fashion.

Courtesy of Team One Advertising and Rhythm & Hues.

Emerging from under the parachute-like car cover, the original Lexus comes into view. This entirely live-action shot sets the stage for the drama to follow.

Courtesy of Team One Advertising and Rhythm & Hues.

The music rises as the wind increases, until suddenly the flapping cover lifts up from the front of the car and blows away, revealing one of the original Lexus models. The voice-over resumes, and as it starts to introduce their new design, the skin of the early-model Lexus begins rippling like the original car cover. The music builds again, the wind rises, until suddenly the whole skin peels away, revealing the latest Lexus design, the ES 300.

In the Beginning

Surprisingly enough, Rhythm & Hues, one of the leading commercial computer graphics studios in Los Angeles, and creators of this advertisement, always begins its creative process with old-fashioned paper and pencil. Whether it is for a television commercial, a feature film special effect, or a theme park ride, each project is first

Slowly, the front of the older Lexus begins to ripple and lift off. To create this effect, both Lexus models were shot live-action at the same time of day on a ranch in Montana.

Courtesy of Team One Advertising and Rhythm & Hues.

carefully story-boarded by hand. They begin in this way in order to distance themselves from the lure of any specific technology, and, therefore, be better able to decide the most appropriate method to use for any given effect.

Thus, when the Lexus ES 300 commercial was presented to them, they immediately produced a series of hand-drawn pictures that defined each scene of the commercial. From this series of drawings, they broke the task down into its basic components. There were essentially six primary elements: an outdoor setting, a car under a cover, the cover blowing off the car, the first shot of an early-model Lexus, the blowing off of that car's skin, and the second shot of a gleaming and shiny Lexus ES 300.

Blown Away to Big Sky Country

At first glance, creating the effect of blowing a car cover off a car while it is sitting in a field may seem simple. But, as with virtually everything in the world of visual illusion, it is far more difficult than it looks. Ideal outdoor environments where the sky, sun, and weather cooperate to perfection are hard to find. In this case, Rhythm & Hues wanted an open country feeling, preferably a ranch setting, with a large, clear horizon and a long sunset. They wanted to shoot the live-action plates of the two automobiles against the reds and oranges of an evening sky. To be assured of enough time to film several takes, they needed to find a place where the sunsets lingered longer than in the Los Angeles area and where the air was clear. After an extensive search, their production scouts found the ideal setting on a ranch in Montana.

The cars, cameras, and crew were shipped to the site, an open rolling pasture with a mountain backdrop. There,

they waited for the perfect sunset to arrive. While waiting, the site was prepared; all the cameras, lights, fans, and car positions were carefully marked out. When the right evening arrived, several shots were taken of the early-model Lexus with the white cover blowing off of it. Then the ES 300 was rolled to the exact same spot and filmed with no extra effects. Without a long sunset, the second car might have had markedly different lighting, thus making the transition between the two difficult, if not impossible. Once the shots were completed and the director satisfied, the crew packed up and went home to begin the computer graphics work.

Why Not Just Blue Screen?

With the computer's capability to extract objects shot against blue screen, you might ask why go to the trouble of an on-location shoot. Why not film the car against blue screen, cut a matte for the car, and then drop in some appropriate background? The reason for this is called blue screen spill. A great deal of trouble is taken to make new cars look as shiny and reflective as possible. When a reflective object is filmed against blue screen, the object mirrors a large amount of blue highlights, regardless of the actual car color. Thus, when the computer tries to extract the blue from the film plate, it will inadvertently remove a good deal of the desired object as well.

Film or television commercial elements are shot against a blue screen in order to extract and later manipulate these elements for a special effect.

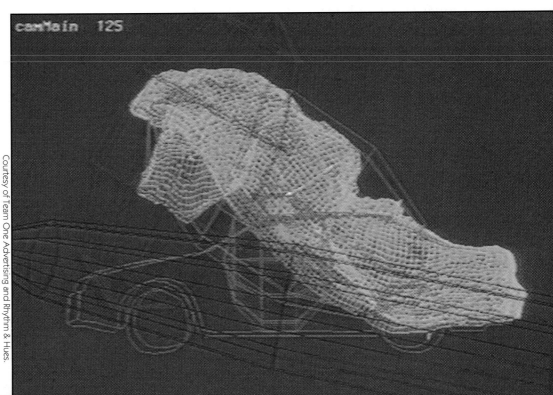

Courtesy of Team One Advertising and Rhythm & Hues.

This image shows one of the various wireframe tests for Rhythm & Hues' digital wind program. They worked in wireframe at this point because it is faster and because they are able to see the precise behavior of the skin more clearly.

Meanwhile, Back at the Studio . . .

Meanwhile, as they waited for the live action to be completed, graphics art director Clark Anderson instructed his team of animators to experiment with the blowing away of the early-model Lexus' skin. First, they examined several more-traditional effects approaches, including airbrushing a real car cover with a painting of the early-model Lexus. They also completed countless tests blowing real car covers off of real cars to give their animators a good understanding of the look of rippling cloth. In turn, these experiments helped them decide that using a real car cover to blow off the skin of the original Lexus just wouldn't give them the feeling they were after. It merely looked like another car cover blowing off, rather than a living creature shedding its skin.

After several other tests, there appeared to be no other choice but computer graphics. Inside the computer, animators built an exact wire-frame model of the ES 300. Concurrently, the best live-action shots of the cars were scanned, frame by frame at high resolution, into the computer. They then cut the image of the early Lexus out of a frame from its live shots and used that cut picture to create the skin for the computer model.

Creating Digital Winds

While the animators were working to create the models and their surfaces, the Research and Development wing of Rhythm & Hues was working on developing a program to simulate wind. They created a physically-based simulation in which various points in the computer model could be seen as being connected by flexible springs. By varying the tension of these springs, different rippling effects could be created. All it took after that was applying the program repeatedly to the constructed model until it blew away in a convincing manner.

Bringing the Elements Together

Once the effect was completed, the elements were composited together and the final print cleaned up. Their elements consisted basically of the first shot of the early Lexus with the real car cover being blown off, a shot of the new Lexus sitting at the same spot in the same field, and a computer animation of the old Lexus blowing away. First, the Rhythm & Hues animators connected the live-action shot of the new ES 300 to the end of the early Lexus' footage. To make the transition between the two pieces of footage, they then composited the computer effect onto the combined films.

Stretching the Cars to Match

Here, two problems arose. The first was that the sizes of the two cars did not precisely match. The older Lexus was a few inches shorter than the new one. To compensate, they used the computer to stretch the skin picture of the old model slightly and then manually smooth the transition between the two cars' sizes in the few frames where it was visible. After they were

Courtesy of Team One Advertising and Rhythm & Hues.

The new ES 300 is clearly visible now. Note the digital shadowing beneath the flapping skin, which is blocking the sunset lighting from hitting the windshield. Techniques such as this heighten the reality of digital imagery.

Courtesy of Team One Advertising and Rhythm & Hues.

The old skin is just an empty husk now. The new car is almost completely in view, and the highlights along the windshield of the new car are there to prove that it too was shot in the same outside environment as the first car.

satisfied with the results, they tackled the second problem, which was anchoring the computer model they had created to the reality of the live-action scene.

Making the Light Look Right

When two objects separate in the real world, the lighting between them is affected. Thus, they could not simply peel away the computer-created skin without somehow changing the lighting, or it wouldn't look real. In this case, they had to make the computer-generated car cover cast a shadow on the real ES 300. Since computer graphic models are created in an imaginary 3-dimensional space, computer shadows can also be generated by lighting the model in that same space and instructing the

computer to create a shadow. After making the shadow, they then extracted it from the computer environment and added it frame by frame to the live-action footage.

With the shadows in place, Rhythm & Hues then made sure the reflections of the live-action sunset on the windows, bumpers, and wheel covers were identical for the two real cars. As you recall, the two cars were shot at slightly different times of day. To be sure there was no sense of discontinuity between them, the Rhythm & Hues animators cut the sunset reflections from the windows of the first car and pasted them onto the windows of the ES 300, completing their work. They delivered their footage on digital tape to the post production house where the voice-over and any final effects were added.

12

Fresca
"Chuckling Straws"

The scene opens showing a table in a garden. On the table are two glasses, each with straws and ice, and one can of Fresca. The voice-over begins, praising the irresistibility of Fresca as a hand pours the can into the glass on the right (the purple straw's glass). As the can empties, the yellow straw in the glass without the Fresca comes to life, sweeping around the rim of its glass until it is facing the other glass. The point of view switches. We look out from inside the yellow straw, as it scans the other glass greedily. The camera cuts to the original view. The yellow straw rears back like a snake and strikes, covering the end of the purple straw.

The drink has just been poured, and the predatory yellow straw is scoping out the situation.

After a brief battle of wills, the yellow straw sucks all the Fresca into its own glass. The victorious straw then chuckles to itself and leans back in its full glass to relax. But in an ominous twist, it is now being scanned by a much larger straw. The camera slowly pulls back to reveal a large empty glass of ice nearby and a hungry red straw stretching itself forward.

Bringing Straws to Life

Clients come to Pixar for character animation. Their history of creating award-winning short films has given them both experience and a well-deserved reputation for excellence in this field. For that reason, most of the commercial work that comes to them is accompanied by only a crude storyboard outline at best. And sometimes, as

© Pixar 1993.

The yellow straw rears back to strike. In the live action, two puppeteers are moving a pair of long straws. The straws needed to be long enough so the puppeteers' hands would be out of sight.

The battle begins. The third puppeteer now begins to pump the Fresca back and forth between the glasses until the yellow straw finally wins. Note the stretching of the flexible straw parts. Subtle animation like this helps to convince the viewer of the intensity of struggle.

Uh Oh! The yellow straw is being scanned by a bigger rival.

with a recent advertisement for Listerine, there is no storyboard at all. Their clients rely on the animators at Pixar to create and execute the story themselves.

> Pixar is a northern California computer animation studio.

In the case of the Fresca advertisement, the basic idea of the story had been roughed out, but it was up to Animation Director Andrew Schmidt, and Technical Director Eliot Smyrl to make it come alive. And they had to complete it in only 2 $\frac{1}{2}$ weeks, less than half their normal 8–10 week production cycle. This gave them one week to film the live action, one week to complete the animation, and 2–3 days to render it all.

Computer Graphics Vs. Live Action

While virtually the entire spot could have been created in computer graphics, the incredibly short time line required that as much of it as possible be shot in live action. Because of this, essentially everything except the tops of the straws was to be filmed on-stage. The props for the live action consisted of the ice, the Fresca, three glasses, three long plastic straws, a pump, and three puppeteers. Tubes were attached out of sight to holes bored in the back of the two glasses, and then run to a pump off-camera, operated by one of the puppeteers.

For the action sequences, two puppeteers moved the straws, whose upper ends protruded past the top of the camera frame. During the sucking scene, the pump pup-peteer worked the liquid back and forth between the glasses to simulate the battle. All of the scenes were shot using a motion control rig in order to capture the exact movements of the camera during each sequence. This motion data was then used to shoot what is called a blank plate and later to supply the movement for the animators' software camera. The blank plate was identical in every way to the live action sequence except that the straws were removed from the glasses, giving a clear background.

After Live Action, Then What?

After the live action was completed, the first step for the animators was to build the 3-dimensional computer environment in which the action was to take place. Since the real environment was simple, this consisted primarily of match-modeling the glasses. To do this correctly, Schmidt's team had recorded every possible measurement they could gather from the live-action set: glass dimensions, distance from camera to the glasses, focal length of the camera lens, distance between the glasses, placements of the lights, and more. Once the glasses were matched and the computer graphics environment constructed, they then scanned in the live-action footage.

Since their task was to animate the parts of the straws above the lips of the glasses, they first had to eliminate these parts from the live action so they could insert their own computer-animated elements. To do this, they created a matte from the match-modeled glasses they had just built and used it to extract the upper part of the blank plate. The straw-free upper section was then overlaid on the live-action footage to provide the background against which they could then animate the straws.

Connecting the Graphics to the Live Action

The next task was to create the connection between their computer graphic straws and the tops of the remaining sections of the straws manipulated by the puppeteers. This was a painstaking, frame-by-frame, pixel-by-pixel task in which the animators had to make sure the computer graphics straw angle and alignment exactly matched the live-action base. Once completed, this provided the

exact motion path of the straws for the upcoming animation.

Just Add Character

Adding character to any object is never an easy task, but when you consider the simplicity of the element that Schmidt had to work with, the believability of the results is remarkable. The shape of the straw lent itself nicely to using a snake metaphor for its actions. The believability, however, came not from how realistically the straw imitated snake behavior, but in how well its actions captured real human emotion, in this case, desire and greed. To aid in developing the human connection, Schmidt created the "periscope" shot through the end of the straw. Here the viewer could immediately see and appreciate the desire for the Fresca building in the straw's mind. This, in turn, added weight to the ferocity and directness of the ensuing attack.

The straw perspective was then echoed in the final scene as the big straw looked down on the chuckling, self-satisfied thief. This last sequence created some interesting new problems because the rim of the glass could no longer serve as the boundary between live action and computer graphics. Here, the point of view is looking down on the inside of the second glass. In this case, the puppeteer manipulated the straw from the bottom of the glass through which a hole had been drilled. The top of the live-action straw extended above the Fresca about half an inch. The same process was used as before to match the movements of the real straw to the computer graphics model; however, they then had to use a special blending program that merged the two images seamlessly.

Finishing Up

With the animation complete, all that remained was the rendering. Here, the precise textures and colors were added as well as film grain, motion blur, and lighting. To be sure the lighting of the computer straws looked exactly like the live action, Schmidt had taken a polished silver ball to the set and filmed it sitting on the table between the glasses. Then he created a computer graphics replica of the silver ball and rendered it. Once the image of the ball was rendered, he could then bring up the picture of the actual ball and compare them. If the lighting on the

The closing scene shows the big, red straw slowly moving forward while the yellow one cowers at the far side of its glass.

two looked identical, he knew the computer lighting was correct.

After the rendering was completed, the elements were digitally composited, and the spot was ready to go to post-production. There, the voice-track was added along with the various special effects to complete the illusion. The final result was an exciting drama of greed and intrigue: a slice of emotion from a straw's-eye point of view.

13

Listerine
"Swinging Bottle"

The spot opens on a wild, green jungle full of ferns, broad leaves, trees, and vines. A rock and roll soundtrack kicks in and a voice-over begins. "It kills germs, just like it always did. . . ." A blue flash zips by from left to right, too fast to make it out. The voice-over continues and a set of words levers up from the jungle: "Fights Plaque . . ."

With a mighty Tarzan swing, the Cool Mint Listerine flies through the jungle. Despite its realism, everything in the picture is computer generated.

Pixar/Colossal Pictures 1992.

The camera pushes past the letters as another blue flash whizzes by in the other direction. It is still too fast to see, but we can see it is hanging from a vine. The rock beat of the music track continues, and, at last, a blue bottle comes sweeping out of the back of the jungle heading straight towards the camera. It is a new blue bottle of Listerine.

A sudden switch of the point of view and we are focused on the label of Cool Mint Listerine. The blurred jungle whips past on either side. The bottle smashes through a series of ferns and then swings up into the sky. Another switch and we are at water level of a cool, blue jungle pond. The Tarzan bottle swings out of the sky, down to the water, splashing water onto the camera lens.

As the lens drips clear, the final shot shows the wild bottle flipping in midair, catching another vine and careening up to a branch where the original gold Listerine bottle is waiting. They bump, as the exuberant blue bottle squashes and stretches. The Gold one watches in amazement; new Cool Mint Listerine has arrived.

Tarzan of the Listerine

Pixar, one of the longtime leaders in character animation, strikes again with a deceptively simple advertisement packed with interesting effects. The advertisement has an air of reality about it, but not a single frame is anything but computer graphics. Pixar's Co-technical directors, Tom Porter and Eliot Smyrl, created its entire world on computer. To begin with, the jungle is an extremely detailed piece of modeling. Producing natural-looking foliage is one of the hardest things to do in computer graphics. With computers, it's easy to makes straight lines and hard edges, but irregular shapes and surfaces, such as those found on trees and bushes, are another story.

If the modelers at Pixar had tried to create this jungle using the standard approach of building each object point by point, they would likely still be at it today. While they do often work this way, software they have developed in-house gives them a little more flexibility. This software allows them to build natural structures procedurally instead of piece by piece or line by line. A *procedure* is a collection of computer commands written in a programming language. In this case, some procedures produced the ferns, some the trees, and others the leaves. The modeler simply has to issue the command, and the computer builds the shape. Once the shape is built it can then be moved, manipulated, and enhanced just like any other model or graphic.

Pixar/Colossal Pictures 1992.

The camera is now focused directly on the bottle, and the viewer is riding along as it swings.

There It Went!

Despite their procedural approach, the jungle still required several weeks to construct in order to get it ready for the animation. Other than the voice-over, the first inkling that there is something interesting happening in this jungle is the series of quick, blue flashes that zip from right to left and left to right across the screen. To establish the depth of the jungle, the first pass happens far away and the second closer.

This blur is something we are used to seeing on live-action film and television. Anything that is moving very quickly past an open camera shutter will create a streak across the film. The length of the streak depends on how fast it is moving, and it happens automatically. In the land of computer graphics, however, this motion blur is not automatic. It is the product of some very heavy calculations during the final rendering stage that translate the speed of the object passing the computer camera into a series of elongated pixels. Despite the cost of these calculations, motion blur is absolutely essential for creating a sense of the real world.

As this ad opens, the blur gets less and less pronounced each time we see it, indicating that the "swinger" is slowing down to our speed. The whole effect produces the feeling that some sort of living creature is coming closer to check us out.

Pop-Up Menus

During this opening section of the ad, different collections of printed ad copy pop up before the camera to announce the benefits of the new product. These were essentially 2-dimensional paintings that were overlaid onto an invisible computer graphics billboard. During the animation process, the billboard was levered up in front of the camera so the words appeared as the camera moved through the jungle. As each billboard came into view, the camera then flew between the letters making them seem as if they, too, had been modeled in three dimensions. This 3-dimensional effect was achieved by adding both transparency and a small amount of motion blur to the letters themselves.

At Last We Meet

On the third pass of the blue Tarzan-like object, we finally see it. The shape of the bottle is distinctively Listerine, even though its bottom half is bent slightly backwards as it holds onto a vine. For everyone familiar with the Tarzan legend, the image is clearly human. As the bottle flashes past, the camera cuts to a full view of the label.

Here Pixar's animators created the feeling of riding along on the vine by mounting the computer camera directly on the bottle. The tail of the vine is shown hanging down the outside edge of the label. To enhance the feeling of motion, the jungle whizzing by on either side is heavily blurred. It's a bit like looking down at the road surface out the side of a moving car. Three times during this sequence, ferns sticking into the path of the swinging bottle are brushed aside.

Out of My Way

Moving the ferns greatly enhances the commercial's realism. Throughout the spot, the jungle scenes are teaming with lush vegetation. From our own experience of walking through woods, we expect to brush the bushes and trees bordering the paths we are using. Yet, if you look closely at virtually every scene in "Swinging Bottle," the bottle touches nothing. However, somehow, we still think it is hitting plants all the time. This feeling is the result of very clever staging created by the three ferns we see hitting the bottle in the shot mentioned above. These three short encounters coming so close together lead our minds to believe that this is happening everywhere.

In addition, even though it looks like the ferns are being casually bumped out of the way by the bottle, every move of each fern frond was animated by hand. If this were filmed in live action, the physics of a real bottle and a real fern would automatically cause this to happen, but in the world of computer graphics this does not happen. If it were not animated to move, the image of the fern would slide right through the middle of the bottle, ruining the illusion of its solidity.

The Wild Blue Yonder

After the label scene, the bottle flies up out of the trees and the camera's point of view suddenly cuts to a placid jungle pond. The blue sky is reflected in the rippling surface of the water as is the surrounding jungle along the shoreline. Out of the blue swings the bottle arcing down until it splashes water onto the camera lens. Everything goes blue and slowly clears as the lens drips dry.

As simple as this scene may seem, it was actually one of the most difficult and time-consuming parts of the commercial, requiring a great deal of time to insure a smooth sense of continuity between the 2- and 3-dimensional effects. The pond and the drip-dry lens were actually fairly easy. The sheet of rippling water was a single, rectangular patch of blue and white, like the sky. Its watery effect was produced in the renderer without any hand

Pixar/Colossal Pictures 1992.

Splashing up computer water.

animation whatsoever. The renderer was simply told to vary the shading of the water over the several frames that were in sight.

In order to maintain a sense of the water's reality, however, the Pixar animators used a nice "cheat." (Cheating in visual effects is not as bad as it sounds. It is the term animators use to describe how they found a nice shortcut around a difficult visual problem.) They never let the camera actually show the water nearest to it. Only middle-range and background water is visible. If the near water had been shown, the complexity of modeling and creating actual water ripples would have increased dramatically.

Similarly, the drip-dry effect was also a snap. It was a 2-dimensional image manipulation trick and required no 3-D animation either. Several frames of the jungle pond were rendered with no action in the scene. Then an image warping procedure was applied to these frames to make them wobble and distort as if waves of liquid were draining down the face of the lens.

The Splash!

The splash, however, was a different story. It consisted of a 9-frame surge of water, followed by a 5-frame splash, and required a major amount of modeling and animation time. For such a few frames, you might think that the effect could have been cut and something more economical inserted, but it was one of the key scenes that drove home the reality of the jungle world and so could not be eliminated.

Swinging Through the Trees

Meanwhile, the blue bottle is off through the jungle again. At one point, it releases its vine, does a flip, and grabs another to head for its final destination. The scene cuts to a horizontal tree branch on which a bottle of the original golden Listerine is sitting. The blue bottle whips up, bounces on the branch, jostling the other. Then, the swinger proceeds to bounce and squash and stretch like an exuberant teenager as the more staid traditional formula looks on.

This last scene also provides a look at some of the subtleties of character animation. It is obvious that the client wanted the new formula to have youth appeal, while still keeping the dignity of the original formula. For this reason, the blue Tarzan bottle squashed, stretched, and bounced in a very exaggerated manner, while the original formula bottle bent only slightly. All the same, this slight bending was just enough to show that gold Listerine was not overly stiff or stuffy.

Creating Character

In this piece, the animators had only the Cool Mint Listerine bottle and the liquid in it from which to fashion a living character. This is minimalist animation at its best. The blue bottle bent in various ways showing its intent as it swung through the jungle. Its pliable nature also gave it a richer organic feel. The liquid inside sloshed back and forth as the bottle moved, enhancing its sense of staging and anticipation. The fluid could have been animated automatically, but then its motion would only have looked like a normal liquid. Once it came under the animator's control, it became part of its character.

The sense of the bottle's individuality was also communicated by the movements of the computer graphics camera which photographed the whole spot. First, the camera moved slowly into the jungle like a wary explorer looking to sight the wild tree-swinger. Then, it rode along with the bottle itself, giving us the exhilaration of whizzing through the trees. Next, it received a splash in the lens, like a pie in the face, showing that the bottle had a sense of humor. And finally, it tracked the swinging bottle as it flipped from vine to vine and landed next to the original formula. Each of these different uses of the camera communicated a different mood and broadened the bottle's sense of character.

The Jungle Revisited

Just how big was this computer jungle? Given the number of different shots, it looks as though the Pixar modelers created the entire Amazon rain forest. Clearly, this could not be true, modeling of any sort is very time-consuming. There must have been a short cut or "cheat" of some sort. The "cheat," in this case, was one of those special bonuses that come for free with computer graphics. Once a computer environment has been created, it can be photographed over and over again from any number of different angles. With live action, on the other hand, all you get is what you film. There is no way to take that imagery and create a new view of the action. If the director wants another shot, all the actors have to re-perform their parts.

In the case of the Listerine jungle, the animators simply used the same set and changed the angle and location of the computer camera. If one scene was shot looking into the jungle from the left side, the next shot was taken looking in from the right. Actually, several different angles were used, making the limited jungle set appear far more expansive than it was.

Coming of Age

Computer animation is capable of almost infinite subtlety. When something is not perfect, an animator or modeler can work on smaller and smaller parts of any given shot until it is. This capability to isolate and control every aspect of a given animation has brought both an increased sense of character and reality to its productions. When simple tin toys can win Oscars (*Tin Toy*, 1988), and Listerine bottles can come alive before our eyes, it is certain that computer animation is coming of age.

14

Exxon: The High Test Tiger

"There is a new gasoline that is clearly advanced . . ." the voice-over begins. A car crests a hill in the background, driving through a winding desert canyon road. Cut to a series of shots showing scientists at work refining a new gasoline product. Cut back to long side-view of the silver-skinned car climbing a second hill. "Who has this gasoline . . .?" continues the voice, just as the front of the car begins to transform itself into a Tiger: "New Phase 4 gasoline from Exxon," as the windows and windshield distort into the stripes of a tiger that is now running in majestic slow-motion strides along the same road.

Shot in Fire Rock Canyon in Nevada, here we see the car moving up a slight incline.

Photos of car transformation to tiger, compliments of Exxon Company, USA, © Exxon Corp. 1994.

A Tiger Test

When an advertising agency approached Pacific Data Images (PDI), one of the leading computer graphics studios, with the idea of transforming a car into a running tiger, everyone thought it was a bit weird. There is so little similarity between the two objects that they weren't sure it would work.

Nick Illyn, PDI's effects director for the piece, thought he first needed to test the feasibility before committing to the project. The agency supplied PDI with some existing footage of a running Exxon tiger and a moving car created for previous advertisements. Illyn's team then cut both the tiger and the car out of this footage and set up a morph between the two. Once the morph sequence was complete, it was composited onto a moving background to see if all the elements would work well together. The test process required two weeks of work, but it showed both the agency and PDI that the concept was good and their approach would get the job done.

This Ain't No Paper Tiger

With proof of concept, it was now time to deal with real tigers. The tiger wrangler, as he is called, who handles the Exxon tiger, was called in to a sound stage in Los Angeles. Exxon keeps four tigers for use in its promotional campaigns. Like the series of dolphins used for the television show "Flipper," each tiger is best for a given set of tricks. PDI ended up using the tiger used most often for face shots because he ran the best.

Unfortunately, he was a male tiger which presented a problem when they went to composite him into the final shot. One thing advertisers do not want in their ads is unintentional sexuality. Flapping animal genitals definitely detract from the impact of the message. For this reason, the chosen tiger had to have his removed with digital surgery so that in the final piece only the sleekness and majesty of his movements would catch the viewer's eye.

Morphing Around
Morphing is the process by which one 2-dimensional image can be smoothly transformed into another. The computer takes each image, and in a series of steps, changes them until they meet at some shape in the middle. The colors are blended in the same way until the change between the two shots is smooth and seamless.

Tigers Against Blue Screen

The sound stage used to film the tigers was one of the largest available in Los Angeles. PDI's film crew needed to be able to capture several strides of the running tiger, which meant they needed at least a hundred-foot stage. Illyn's crew built a ramp that long and covered it and the background against which the tiger would be filmed in blue screen. Overhead, they hung two mammoth *fisher boxes* for lighting. Fisher boxes are most often used to light the cars in automobile advertisements because they provide a bright, uniform, and diffuse light.

> Blue screen is what film elements are shot against in order to be able to composite them into various special effects shots. The blue background is automatically removed by the computer leaving only the object or actor that was filmed. It is essential for most image morphing.

The tiger wrangler then brought his charge to the end of the ramp. He gave his assistant a head start and then released the tiger, who went bounding along the stage after him. The tiger could get in almost eight full strides in the space available, which would probably give them enough to pull out the two to three they needed for the effect. The tiger was filmed with high speed cameras shooting at both 96 and 100 frames per second. For the final commercial, they ended up using the 96 frame-per-second shots and doubled them up to make it even slower. Doubling means they simply showed the same frame twice which extended a two-second movement of the tiger into a 4-second movement.

Out to the Desert

With the tiger under wraps, Illyn was ready to film the main body of the commercial, a car driving through a desert canyon. For this footage he took his crew out to Fire Rock Canyon near Las Vegas, a rugged setting of fiery, red rock walls and ledges. Their most difficult shot was the section of footage required for the morph sequence.

Since they were going to have to do some fancy composite work later, they knew they had to capture several passes of the same scene. This meant using a motion-control camera. Their approach here was different from the way motion-control rigs are normally used. The standard approach is to create the movement of the camera on

Photo of car transformation to tiger, compliments of Exxon Company, USA,
© Exxon Corp. 1994.

The tiger morph has begun, working its way from the front bumper to the back of the car.

computer and then let the computer control the camera. In this case, however, they let a human cameraman control the first pass while the computer recorded what he did.

This meant that as the car drove up the hill at a precise speed, the cameraman had the freedom to act as if this were any other live-action shoot, panning and tilting the camera to get the best shots possible. Having a human direct the camera allows for much more creative spontaneity than when a preprogrammed computer is in control. After he was satisfied with his filming of the car, the captured data could be used to drive the camera on the next two passes.

Have Blue Screen, Will Travel

They needed to capture the next passes before the light changed, and so immediately upon completing the car shot, the background plate was created. This involved simply letting the motion camera repeat the first pass without the car in the scene. This background plate

Photo of car transformation to tiger, compliments of Exxon Company, USA, © Exxon Corp. 1994.

Photos of car transformation to tiger, compliments of Exxon Company, USA, © Exxon Corp. 1994.

At last, we see the tiger alone and the morph is complete.

would be used later for compositing the morph sequence and a section of the foreground.

Once this shot was complete, the final pass could begin. One of the interesting aspects of this ad was that the car-to-tiger morph had to take place while the car passed behind a series of low-lying rocks and vegetation. It is quite natural for elements in the foreground to partially block the view of a moving car, but it is not easy to deal with this when creating a special effect. Somehow the foreground elements had to be isolated so they could later be layered back on top of the effect once it was set into the *background plate*.

A background plate is a shot of the empty scene (no actors, no live action) using the same camera motion as was used in the live action.

What makes this morph unique is the successful combination of two very dissimilar images, the tiger and the car.

To accomplish this task, PDI created the world's first mobile blue screen. They built a blue-screen billboard about forty feet long and attached it to the side of a moving van, completely hiding the truck itself. The screen came down to within a few inches of the road surface to be sure to catch all the low-lying vegetation. The truck's driver was then instructed to drive the truck over the same stretch of road at the same speed as the car. It proved difficult for the driver to maintain the required speed, and so the car drove directly in front of it out of the film frame to give him a point of reference.

Blue Screen Spill

Blue screen spill is what happens when some of the color of the background screen reflects off the foreground element being photographed. When the computer goes to remove the blue screen automatically, it can't tell the difference between the blue of the screen and the reflected blue on the object being shot. Thus, it will remove both, leaving holes or ragged edges in the object. Since cars are primarily lit by reflection, the blue of the background screen would show up all over its surface.

Changing a Car into a Tiger

With the blue screen shot of the foreground complete, the effect could now be assembled. The first step was to create the morph itself. This meant first creating a series of mattes that would cut both the car from the original outdoor shot, and the tiger out of their original footage. The tiger was easy. Since it was shot against blue screen on a sound stage, the computer could pluck it out automatically.

The car, on the other hand, was more difficult. Since it is virtually impossible to shoot a car against blue screen because of what is called *blue screen spill*, each frame of the car sequence had to be cut by hand on the computer. Once the elements of the car and the tiger had been isolated, they could then begin creating the morph.

The primary difficulty here lay in the vast dissimilarity between the tiger and the car. They shared no common features. While the morphing process certainly handled the transformation all right, it didn't look very convincing. It actually looked more like a dissolve between two images, where the first image of the car slowly faded to reveal the second image of the tiger in its place. Somehow, the two elements had to be more closely connected to make it seem more believable.

Here, Illyn decided to make more use of the blackness of the windshield and window glass. By changing the morphing pattern of the car's glass, he was able to make the windows transform themselves to match the blackness and placement of the stripes on the tiger's body. After a few tests of his new idea, he saw that it worked purr-fectly. There was no mistaking that the car was transforming itself into a living tiger.

Laying in the Effects

With the morph sequence completed, it was time to composite all the elements. First, the foreground elements had to be extracted from the mobile blue screen pass. The computer was able to handle almost all of this automatically with a few manual touch-ups. From this, they could create a matte to remove the foreground of the blank plate. On top of this, they then layered the morphing car sequence followed by the extracted foreground elements. The final results showed the car driving along the road and transforming into the tiger as it passed behind the various rocks and shrubs in the foreground. This total effect lasted no more than four seconds out of the entire commercial, but it was the key element that drove home its message.

Moxy, a Dog of a Different Color

On the day after Thanksgiving, 1993, Moxy performed live and in color over worldwide television. At the top of every hour throughout the day, his manic antics were broadcast from the Turner Network studios in Atlanta, Georgia, over the Cartoon Network, reaching audiences across North America, Latin America, and Europe. He laughed, he joked, and he was a resounding success.

Introducing Moxy's Pirate TV Show! Moxy, the first all-digital cartoon character with its own TV show, hams it up in his live-action set.

"Moxy" produced by Colossal Pictures in association with the Cartoon Network.

Moxy was created against a computer blue screen, making it easy to extract him from the background and composite him into the live action.

Moxy doing a dance number.

Not Another Performing Animal!

In this age of instant global communications, there is nothing new or even interesting about either a performing dog or a worldwide audience. Unless, of course, you happen to be a pooch like Moxy. His pedigree says he is a 100%, pure-bred, computer-generated, and computer-animated mutt. The first and best of his breed, he is the new mascot for Turner Network Television's Cartoon Network.

Real time is the actual time passing on the clock. Most animations require months to create the character movements. Real time animations are those that are created on the spot.

Not just another performing animal, Moxy is the product of six months of intensive computer modeling and programming, and requires a minimum staff of three humans to come alive in *real time*. Real time animation is one of the

"Moxy" produced by Colossal Pictures in association with the Cartoon Network.

hottest areas of computer graphics, requiring the fastest hardware, the sleekest software, and lots of know-how to pull it off right.

Building a Digital Dog

Shortly after Brad DeGraff joined Colossal Pictures in San Francisco, he and Colossal Pictures approached The Cartoon Network with the idea of creating an animated mascot for them. This character would appear between cartoons, tell a few jokes, and then introduce the next cartoon, much the way human emcees used to operate on the weekday, after-school children's programs of the sixties and early seventies.

Human Motion Capture

Human movements can be captured by computer in a number of different ways. Some involve mounting magnetic sensors on an actor and then tracking the sensors as they move through a strong magnetic field. Others use highly reflective Ping-Pong balls taped to a performer's body, and videotape the performer with several high-speed cameras. Whatever the approach, it is possible to collect motion information and then apply that motion to a 3-dimensional computer model.

What DeGraff and Colossal Pictures proposed was to create a 3-dimensional computer graphics mascot who would use *captured human motion* and recorded voice to give it a look like nothing else on television. Using a standard 2-dimensional cartoon character would not work, because it would not have a strong enough identity of its own. Such a character would simply blend in to the string of cartoons that surrounded it.

The Cartoon Network loved the idea, and contracted them to produce sixteen interstitial animations of between 30 and 45 seconds each. DeGraff originally wanted to create not only Moxy himself, but also his set in computer graphics. Due to budgetary constraints, however, it was determined that only Moxy would be created by computer. The set was to be live-action, and the digital dog would later be composited into place.

More Cartoon than Computer Graphic

Even though Moxy is a computer graphics character, with the potential of 3-dimensional realism, he is cartoon character through and through. His arms and legs have no joints, but rather are flexible tubes that can vibrate and bend anyway they please. His facial features are skewed the way standard cartoon characters often are so his eyes can appear on the same side of his nose. And his "office" is loaded with cartoon logic: all the heaviest and most dangerous objects are precariously perched on the highest shelves, waiting for the slightest excuse to fall.

Creating Moxy's Character

Once the computer model of Moxy was complete and the live-action set was built, the real work of creating his character could begin. Now they had to decide how Moxy would move, what his voice would sound like, and how he would best be shown on camera. Because of real-world television budgets, they were limited to a three-camera shoot, which meant that only three fixed views of Moxy were possible. Each view, however, could be either tight, medium, or wide, coupled with a series of other options that included either blurred or sharp focus. Overall, about 20 different backgrounds were created, with enough variety to keep the pieces interesting.

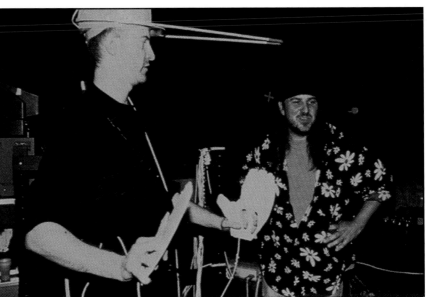

Comedian Bobcat Goldthwait, standing by actor John Stevenson, is ready to perform Moxy's voice.

"Moxy" produced by Colossal Pictures in association with the Cartoon Network.

"Moxy" produced by Colossal Pictures in association with the Cartoon Network.

Motion sensors to capture the actor's movements are not only mounted on various parts of his body, but also on the long beak of his hard hat and on the tips of the hand cutouts.

I see what you're saying

Lip synching is one of the more tedious tasks in computer animation, usually involving careful frame-by-frame manipulation of the character's mouth. Once it is completed, it is fixed forever because any changes in the sound track means the lip-synch process has to start all over again. With Moxy, this is not so. He comes equipped with a computer-based lip synching system that takes care of virtually all his lip movements automatically. It is based primarily on sound volume, which makes his mouth open wider for louder sounds. For the director, this provided a great deal more freedom to change the story when needed.

Tell Me a Storyboard

To begin the process, a paper storyboard was created for each of the pieces. From this, the live action crew then determined what shots would be needed of Moxy's physical set. Inside the computer, there were three graphics cameras identically matched to those on the live action set. When activated, they would film Moxy in exactly the same way the live-action crew filmed his set. Thus, when

Moxy was finally composited into the live action, it would look as though both he and the set had been filmed by the same cameras.

Once the shots were determined, it was time to create the voice track. Colossal Pictures hired comedian Bobcat Goldthwait to create Moxy's grave but child-like voice. This was then combined with an electronic version of the storyboard to give the actor who would be creating Moxy's movements a good idea of the timing.

Grab Me Some Motion

To bring life to Moxy, actor John Stevenson suited up in a magnetic motion capture harness that strapped sensors on his limbs, torso, and head. Since Moxy's hands and nose were extra long, the actor wore a hard-hat with a long beak and a pair of large cardboard cutout hands that he could slip onto his fingers. Extra sensors were mounted at the ends of the hard-hat beak and the cardboard hands to capture the movements for Moxy's digital nose and hands.

As the actor moved, he could see Moxy moving the same way on a monitor in front of him. Their movements weren't exactly the same because Moxy's motion software was written to distort his arms and legs slightly so they would seem more rubbery than real. To give the actor an even greater feeling for Moxy's evolving character, the sound track had already been lip-synched to Moxy's mouth movements by the time the motion capture began.

In addition to the lip-synched sound track and his view of Moxy on the monitor, the actor also had the electronic storyboard posted in front of him. This provided both the timings of each shot along with what is called the edit decision list. The edit decision list is a chronological listing of every cut point, camera change, or scene change and when they take place. This meant that the actor could anticipate camera changes in his movements, using them much the same way a newscaster does when he or she turns to face a different camera. The list also told him when to reach his hands out as if he were touching something in the live set.

The overall effect of performing Moxy in this way produced a set of extremely believable and fluid motions, that fit with both the voice track and the live-action set. Remarkably, an animation process that would have required weeks or even months using the standard keyframe approach was completed in a matter of a few days.

Tuning Up the Results

Performing Moxy's animation instead of drawing it allowed DeGraff's team to capture almost 95% of the movements they thought they needed to bring Moxy to life. The finishing touches came from a set of programs (groups of instructions in computer software) that supplemented the performed movements, and a small amount of manual tweaking. The manual work was not the usual key frame animation described earlier in the book. It was, rather, a different set of performances controlled by either the keyboard or by joysticks.

Using these devices, the animators added various special movements, such as squinting his eyes, raising his eyebrows, or crinkling his mouth to what they had already captured. These new effects could simply be layered onto the existing animation by tapping into the channels that controlled each of those body parts.

The software-induced movements, on the other hand, included a raft of other more subtle effects that added an almost subliminal feeling of life to Moxy. There were computer routines that blinked his eyes and wiggled his ears, as well as programs that made him breathe, move his hands and fingers, and bend his feet up from the floor as he walked. Each of the extra motions helped eliminate the stark stiffness that often plagues computer animations.

Putting Moxy in His Place

Once Moxy had been satisfactorily brought to life, it was time to composite him into the live action. The matching computer cameras were instructed to capture Moxy's actions just as if they had been shot with the corresponding live-action camera. From these individual frames, black-and-white mattes were created to block out the part of the live-action shot that would be hidden if Moxy had actually been there. Then, the digital frames containing Moxy were layered onto those of the live action, bringing him out of the digital world and into the "real" world of television video.

The final results were a series of amazingly convincing performances that looked as if the entire production had somehow been created on the live-action stage.

"Moxy" produced by Colossal Pictures in association with the Cartoon Network.

In a classic cartoon pose, Moxy holds a lighted stick of dynamite.

16

Automobile Under Glass: The Mitsubishi Magnifying Glass

The scene opens inside a gleaming laboratory. As the voice-over begins, describing the latest Mitsubishi automobile, a huge 8-foot magnifying glass swings into place beside the car. The lens moves slowly around the polished body revealing each feature in magnified detail as it is described by the voice-over. Not a single fault is to be found, even under such close scrutiny. Satisfied lab personnel in white smocks jot down notes on the car's perfection as the glass passes first down one side, then across the front, and to the back of the car, bringing the ad to a close.

The giant magnifying glass distorts the image so believably that no one would think it wasn't real. To create the effect, several steps from digital preplanning to compositing the computer-generated magnification were required.

Courtesy of Grey Advertising and Rhythm & Hues.

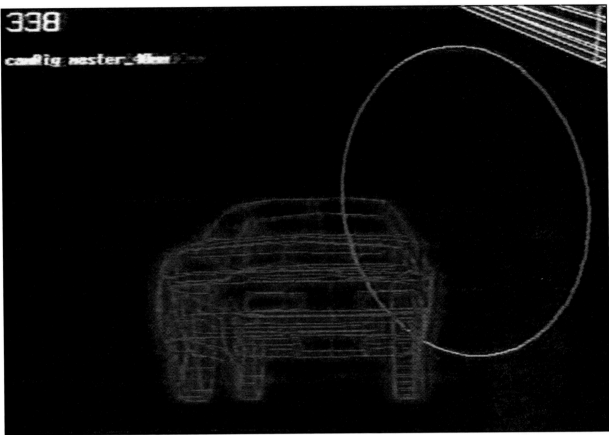

Courtesy of Grey Advertising and Rhythm & Hues.

This shows a wireframe image of the car plus a circle for the magnifying glass. These images were used to help find the best motion paths for the camera and the glass.

How They Did It

This deceptively simple advertisement, created by Rhythm & Hues, one of the leading commercial computer graphics studios in Los Angeles, was the product of meticulous planning that made extensive use of the computer's capability to previsualize what they were trying to create. As is often typical in this industry, the agency creating the ad approached Rhythm & Hues with a fairly well-defined concept, but with no idea how they might execute it. It was obvious from the start that creating a real 8-foot magnifying lens would be out of the question. This size glass is as large as some astronomical observatory lenses and would require months to cast and grind at the cost of several hundred thousand dollars.

First Build the Set . . . Digitally

To come up with a solution, the Rhythm & Hues creative director on this piece, Charles Gibson, sat down at the computer with the commercial's director and constructed a computer graphic model of the entire spot. They knew the size of the car and so built everything on the set to match that scale. Then, using only the comput-

er model, they created several different versions of the commercial, testing camera angles, set configurations, lighting, and camera moves on computer.

In the course of their explorations, they discovered that it would be best to create everything in real form for live-action filming except the lens inside the magnifying glass. Once this was decided, they then realized that instead of using just one motion-control system to move the camera around the car, they really needed two, one for the camera and one for the magnifying glass hoop.

> Motion control systems are computer-driven devices that automatically move a camera or a set prop on a specific path through a live-action set.

The previsualization tests also brought a series of other benefits. The first was that they could create the set design, develop the action of the piece, and have it all approved by their client before beginning actual set construction. Then they could simply extract the construction plans already assembled on computer. Additionally, they knew ahead of time what specific areas

Courtesy of Grey Advertising and Rhythm & Hues.

Here, the empty hoop is filmed moving around the car on the live-action stage. The computer effects will be composited inside the hoop later.

of the set needed special attention and what could be ignored based on the computer-created camera move. For example, a large section of the laboratory ceiling did not have to be constructed because they knew the camera would never look in that direction.

They simply took the existing mathematical data from the computer model and fed them to the computers that drove the actual motion-control rigs on the set.

The Near-Optimal Path

Once the props had been built, the advertisement was ready for filming. Here again, the previsualization supplied some very key components. Since they had already worked out the motion paths for both the camera and the empty magnifying hoop, they did not have to spend time on the live action set figuring out the optimal camera path.

Courtesy of Grey Advertising and Rhythm & Hues.

The construction specifications for the magnifying hoop were created on computer first during the preplanning stage.

While not absolutely perfect, the previsualized motion paths provided a very close approximation of what they wanted. In areas where it was not exactly right, they simply intervened and created the move they were after. This new data was then fed back into the computer graphics system for later use in creating the effect.

Three Separate Camera Passes

In this case, they used the motion data to complete three separate camera passes on the live-action set. The first pass moved both the magnifying bezel and the camera. The camera was using a lens with a wide field of view that allowed the entire car to be visible during the entire move. The second pass used the same camera, but a piece of opaque backing was placed inside the bezel. From this pass, the computer could extract a matte that would show exactly where the magnifying glass lens was passing at any time. The third pass moved only the camera, which was then outfitted with a telephoto lens to give an extreme close-up of the car's features.

The reason for the last shot was to ensure the reality of the magnification in the final commercial. It is possible to take a section of any image and blow it up on computer, but in the process you lose detail. In this case, they decided to shoot the car with a powerful enough lens so the image would lose nothing in translation. To be certain they were getting the best close-up shot, they created a real-time video system that allowed them to see only the section of the image that would be shown in the glass. They did this by creating a matte from the matte pass described earlier and then passing that matte over the third pass imagery as it was being taken. Using this approach, they could make minor camera adjustments on the fly.

Cheating the Magnifying Lens

Once all the passes were completed, the film was scanned into the computer for compositing. Since the magnified car footage was basically a flat image, Rhythm & Hues used a software tool they had developed earlier to create

Courtesy of Grey Advertising and Rhythm & Hues.

The first pass with the empty hoop is shown on a monitor with the second pass overlaid on it. The second pass used a telephoto lens to create the close-up footage. The computer will then stretch the inside image out to the edges of the hoop.

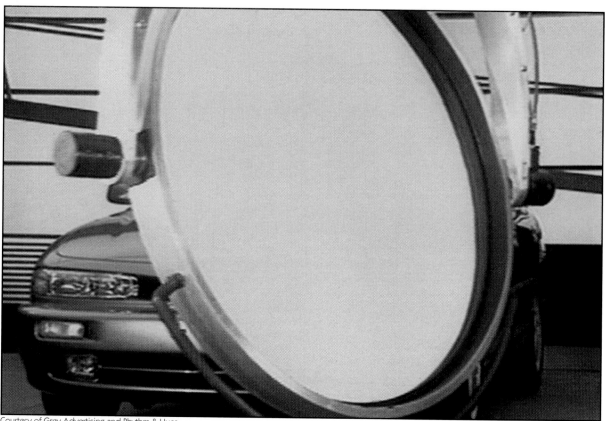

Courtesy of Grey Advertising and Rhythm & Hues.

Before the final image can be composited inside the hoop, whatever was inside the hoop has to be removed. A matte is then created that is the size of the hoop and moved over the digital imagery created for the interior. This selects the right part of the digital image, then that is placed inside the magnifying hoop to finish the ad.

the bending effect that would normally be seen in a lens. Their distortion algorithm was based on actual lens physics, so it was initially a very faithful representation of what you would see. The agency, however, thought it distorted the product too much. They wanted an effect that bent the view of the car at the edges of the lens, but left it intact in the middle.

This was easy to resolve, since the computer offers virtually complete control over the images involved. They merely changed some parameters in their software, and the results were as we now see them in the accompanying pictures.

All that remained after this was to add both the reflections and the highlights that we expect to see on a piece of glass and to tweak the look of a couple of the features of the actual car. The reflections helped to anchor the computer imagery in the reality of the live-action laboratory, and the adjusted features made the car seem that much more appealing to the viewers. Once this all was complete, the piece was then sent to a post-production house for the addition of the sound track and any final 2-D visual effects.

17

From the Past to the Future: The Secrets of the Luxor Pyramid

A startling discovery has just been made. Deep beneath the surface of the planet, the remains of an ancient civilization have been discovered along with powerful new technologies that will revolutionize the world. The archaeologist in charge has just broken the hieroglyphic code which tells her that a unique crystal obelisk lies at the heart of it all. But there is evil afoot. Both the military and a group of future society fanatics, headed by the cunning genius Osiris, want to capture this obelisk and its accompanying power for themselves.

Liquid figures emerge from a silvery blue circle of water that is the origin of life. The entire dream sequence was computer generated and shown in stereoscopic projection.

Future Meets the Past

Thus begins the simulated adventure at the Luxor Las Vegas Hotel in Las Vegas, where three separate film-based attractions have recently been installed. Created for Circus Circus by special effects wizard Douglas Trumbull, best known for his remarkable effects on films like *2001: A Space Odyssey, Star Trek* (the movie), and *Blade Runner,* the attractions include a thrilling simulator ride, a visit to a live-seeming talk show, and a trip into a series of horrifying and magnificent views of the future.

The fun begins with a trip two miles beneath the surface of the earth that involves riding in two separate motion-based simulators. The first is a rough-hewn construction elevator, whose hydraulics and actuators give the feeling of smooth descent. Suddenly, the evil Osiris cuts the elevator cable and the cab free-falls. The riders feel the acceleration as the cab picks up speed. Fortunately, the heroes, Carina and Mac, are in the neighboring cab, and at

incredible risk to themselves, jam a piece of metal beneath the falling cab, which screeches to a halt just before it hits the bottom.

Attraction One

The first Luxor Las Vegas Hotel attraction, "In Search of the Obelisk," is a simulator ride, much like the "Back to the Future" and "Star Tours" rides found at the Universal Studios and Disneyland theme parks. The plot revolves around a crystal obelisk found in the ruins of an ancient civilization two miles beneath the surface of the earth. It is the source of power for the advanced levitation technologies discovered in the ruins. The heroes, Mac and Carina, want to keep the dig and its artifacts open to the public, while the government and a futurist fanatic named Osiris want it for themselves. The simulator attraction is a high-speed chase through the caverns below, as Mac, one of the archaeologist heroes, tries to recover the obelisk from Osiris and free his kidnapped colleague Carina.

With an audible sigh of relief, the audience exits the first ride and then enters the main simulator bays. Here, the real action begins as Mac tries to pilot everyone back to the surface while chasing Osiris, who has just kidnapped Carina. As the simulator platform flings its riders back-and-forth and up-and-down, Mac flies through an enormous computer-generated underground cavern, dodging rockets and explosions as Osiris' ship and the military VTOL (Vertical Take-Off and Landing) craft battle it out in a high-tech dogfight.

High Tech Drama

The drama and the ride are wild, and the digital effects thoroughly engrossing. This first film in the Luxor trilogy actually lasts only four minutes, but because of its intensity seems far longer. It is one of the growing number of film-based attractions that are offering audiences more than just a passive viewing experience; and it is part of a new participatory entertainment phenomenon that would not have been possible without the precisely coordinated interaction of live performance, live-action film, computer graphics, and digitally controlled motion platforms.

The Trumbull Company's motion-control camera photographs one of the miniature sets for the simulator ride, "In Search of the Obelisk."

(Photo by Drew Zelman) © 1993 The Trumbull Company.

This live-action shot of the heroes in the neighboring elevator cab will be composited with a photographed miniature background that makes it appear as if they are racing downward alongside the audience's plummeting cab.

The Roots

It all began when Circus Circus (one of the largest hotel and casino owners in Las Vegas) decided to build a spectacular glass pyramid hotel in Las Vegas. To match the exotic exterior, they turned to Douglas Trumbull, also known as the father of the modern simulator ride, to create the inside effects. He came up with the triple attraction theme mentioned above and the project got under way. From the start, Trumbull knew he would need computer special effects, and so he, in turn, hired the Hollywood-based Kleiser-Walczak Construction Co.

The production schedule was extremely tight, allowing only sixteen months to create all three films from start to finish, but Kleiser-Walczak saw the project as a golden opportunity to expand into new areas. They immediately agreed to set up a primary graphics installation inside Trumbull's headquarters located a continent away in Lennox, Massachusetts. Like the first wave of marines assaulting a beachhead, the company trucked in their gear, parachuted in over 20 staff members, and had their network of 25 Silicon Graphics workstations up and running over a single weekend. To this heavy-hitting configuration were later added three Power Visualization

System (PVS) supercomputers by IBM, each of which had 32 high-speed processors and over two gigabytes of memory.

Knowing they had to hit the ground running, they also hired a group of accomplished senior computer animators, each of whom had at least five years "in the trenches" of high-pressure production. These animators formed the cores of the three needed graphics teams: one for the past, "In Search of the Obelisk," one for the present, "Luxor Live?" and one for the future, "Theatre of Time."

Diving into the Past: "In Search of the Obelisk"

"In Search of the Obelisk" is a masterful combination of live action, motion-control model shots, and computer graphics. There is one minute of full computer-graphics animation in the simulator ride, plus an additional minute and a half of computer effects composited onto the live action during the rest of the film. In looking at these small numbers, it is tempting to ask what the excitement is all about. After all, the genesis effect created for *Star Trek II* back in 1982 was over a minute long.

The Luxor films (ranging from 5 to 25 minutes long) are actually unique in many ways. Trumbull has always pushed the frontier of filmmaking to its limits wherever he could, and this project was no different. In this case, for the first film he used high-speed film projection technology that he had invented and an extra-large film size. With this, he projected the first film at 48 frames per second, twice the normal theater projection rate to create an extremely bright and much more life-like image. Additionally, the film was projected onto a 30-foot-in-diameter simulation dome, inside of which sat the simulator motion platform. The dome provided almost a 180 degree view of the action from every seat.

All of this meant that the computer graphics had to be created at super-high resolutions and for twice as many film frames as would normally be required. The other attractions had similar unique requirements that demanded far more labor in the digital fields than seems immediately apparent.

The Underground Cavern

The simulator ride opens with Mac hooking his monolev vehicle up to the audience's simulator platform by mistake. He is in a hurry to catch Osiris, who has just kid-napped Carina, and thinks he is hooking up to a group of his own men. By the time he notices the error, it is too late, and the action has begun. Trumbull filmed both Mac and the sled in live action against blue screen, later compositing it over the model and computer graphics shots.

> The monolev vehicle was one of the advanced technologies discovered in the ancient ruins. It runs on an unknown levitational technology.

For the action plate, Trumbull had originally planned to create everything except the flying vessels using miniature models shot with his own motion-control system. He discovered, however, that for one shot in particular this would be prohibitively expensive. The shot lasted approximately one minute and involved flying through the massive underground cavern that housed the previous civilization.

Because of the rapid changes in scale required by the shot, Trumbull realized he would have needed to build a huge, highly detailed model, which would have cost him far more than creating it all on computer. Thus, the

The audience is attached to Mac's monolev vehicle, like it or not. As they race through the underground cavern, an assailant drops onto Mac's monolev to throw him off Osiris' trail.

animation team for the past, headed by Derry Frost, added that shot to the group it was already creating.

Made from Scratch

The giant cavern took shape through the close collaboration of Trumbull art director Tom Valentine and Derry Frost. There were no physical mock-ups constructed to guide them, and the work was done directly on the computer. The most difficult aspect of creating the cavern was somehow conveying a sense of its immensity. For this, they looked at hundreds of pictures of giant man-made structures, such as the Hoover dam and various skyscrapers, to see how light and texture communicated the right sense of scale.

Once they found the right visual cues, they then had to consider how to light such an enormous space. Here again, they turned to their reference libraries and gradually evolved the idea of painting the computer lights directly on the cavern surfaces themselves. This completely eliminated the difficulties inherent in trying to light the whole space with a selection of directed computer lights.

During the simulator ride "In Search of the Obelisk," Mac takes the audience diving into the vast underground cavern where Osiris is caught in a dogfight.

What are the Walls Made Of?

Because the audience was going to be so close to the viewing screen, and because of their 180 degree view of the imagery, the walls along the entire length of the cavern had to be detailed and variable. Their look could not simply repeat a pattern like the background in a Saturday morning cartoon.

By the same token, the expense of creating unique surfaces throughout the entire cavern prohibited using this approach. Frost and his team remedied this situation by doing a little of each. Patterns of surface textures were, in fact, repeated over and over across the walls; however, the computer was used to optimally place the patterns and to distort each in its own unique way. The result was the appearance of infinite variability at a price they could afford.

After careening through the underground digital cavern, Mac takes the simulator audience through a harrowing field of gigantic computer-generated, swinging obelisks that guard the entrance to the underground pyramid.

Ships, Rockets, and Monolevs

The ships also suffered from the same scaling problems as the cavern. At times, they were shown from far away, and at times, they were close enough to see inside and catch sight of the instrument panels and the names on the soldiers' jerseys. The original models were first built in balsa wood, after the Trumbull creative staff previsualized them on their computers. These models were then digitized with a 3-D digitizer to create the beginning computer elements.

> Previsualization is the process of using a computer to create pictures of something before it has been created in the real world. 3-D digitizers are used to convert real 3-dimensional objects into computer graphic models.

Once the models were built inside the computer, it was time to create their surface look. This was largely left up to the creativity of the animators, with regular feedback from Trumbull and his staff. Since the level of detail required by each shot was so highly variable, the animators had to create the surfaces as if they would be shown close up at any time. This meant producing hundreds of surface textures from the treads on the fighters' tires, to the rivets on the wings, to various transparency filters that affected how light played across the metallic surfaces. For the military VTOL, this amounted to an amazing 256 megabytes of digital data.

Moving Them Through the Models

These ship models were used both in the cavern scene which was 100 percent digital, as well as in subsequent footage where they mixed with motion-control model shots. One of the primary considerations with the models' shots was matching the computer graphics lighting to that used on-stage.

Since the model sets were filmed using Trumbull's motion-control gantry, matching the lighting was not as difficult as it could have been. After the live-action pass was completed, a Ping-Pong ball was attached directly below the camera lens, and the rig was sent through the set once more. Frost's team then took the film footage of the Ping-Pong ball and were able to deduce the way the lighting worked during each frame of the pass by watching the highlights change on the ball.

Attraction Two

The story begun in the first attraction is further developed in the second, "Luxor Live?" Here, a television host interviews the characters of the previous story about the importance of the obelisk. Carina, who escaped from Osiris in the first film, is back down in the underground dig, and she has had a premonition that something amazing is soon to be revealed to her. As earthquakes strike the surface of the planet, upsetting the television show, Carina goes into a trance, and a brilliant dream sequence of images about the origin and the future of life begins. The attraction ends with the end of her vision.

Once they had this information, they then built digital "light cubes" around each of the flying ships. They positioned computer lights at each of the cube's corners and then varied the intensities of the lights according to the changes recorded during the Ping-Pong ball pass. This gave them an exact match so that the computer elements could then be seamlessly integrated into the live action film.

Projecting the Image

The simulator domes onto which the imagery was projected were almost exactly hemispherical. To compensate for the bend in the screen, all the live-action footage was shot using a fish-eye lens so that when the image was projected on the curved screen it looked straight. This was no problem for the live action, but it tripled the challenge of the computer graphics.

A computer graphics lens of the exact same distortion had to be created inside the computer. Kleiser-Walczak's head of software development, Frank Vitz, set to work on this, and with

detailed input from the makers of the actual fish-eye lens, produced the needed program. It required, however, that each frame of computer animation be rendered three separate times, one using a left view, one straight ahead, and one using a right view. The program then took each of these views and combined them to synthesize the final image. By the time they finished with the sequence, the simple one-minute shot of the cavern had taken over one month to produce.

Dealing with the Present: "Luxor Live?"

The second attraction in the Luxor Las Vegas Hotel extravaganza is not a simulator ride, but it is an entirely simulated experience. The audience is brought into what looks like a live television studio, where they watch and participate in the interview of the characters seen in the first attraction.

The interview is actually on film, but it is so lifelike that, at times, it is easy to forget you are watching a film. The film itself is rear projected onto a screen on the stage below, at the rate of 60 frames a second. This makes the image so bright that it looks like live theater. To enhance the appearance of realism, there are also live stagehands going through the motions of putting on a real show, as well as pieces of furniture that seem to protrude from the screen images themselves.

Liquid figures emerge from a silvery blue circle of water that is the origin of life. The entire dream sequence was computer generated and shown in stereoscopic projection.

The figures evolve into dancing couples made of glass.

The Digital Dream

The talk show contains no digital imagery or effects, but there is a remarkable sequence of stereographic imagery towards the end of the show. Carina, the female archaeologist kidnapped and saved in the earlier film, is shown back underground at the dig. She is expecting an auspicious event when suddenly she goes into a trance. The audience sees the contents of her trance vision on a film screen above the talk show stage.

Previously, the audience had been given 3-D movie glasses with the warning that something was about to happen for which they needed protective eye wear. Just before the sequence begins, they are told to put them on, and the stereographic computer dream sequence comes spilling out from the screen and virtually into their laps.

But fear overtakes them, and they become armored. Instead of dancing, they fight to an explosive conclusion.

The Primal Origin

Carina's vision is a series of images that capture the evolution of life from its very beginnings to its own destruction in a fiery blast. The heart of the piece is a series of rich images showing two silvery figures rising slowly out of a reflective pool of water. They are dancing to a haunting melody as they slowly form into a man and a woman. As they take shape, they solidify into two glass figures that joyously dance around each other. Other glass couples can be seen in the background.

The dance progresses, but sadly, things start to go wrong. The dancing couples become afraid of one another and cover themselves in armor. Soon, instead of dancing, they are fighting to the same music, until, rising to a crescendo, the figures come together and are destroyed in a fiery atomic blast.

Getting the Rhythm

The glass figures are the most recent additions to Kleiser-Walczak's stable of Synthespians. These are computer-generated human characters whose motions are captured directly from real humans. In this case, two dancers, a man and a woman, were filmed dancing to the film's music.

The system they used to capture the dancers' movements was not powerful enough to deal with two performers at once, and so each had to be filmed separately. The female dancer performed first, and the male then danced to a video reproduction of her movements. Each of them wore a series of reflective balls on key parts of their bodies and were filmed by a bank of six high-speed video cameras. The recorded motions of the balls were then automatically translated into 3-D movement data that could be applied to the computer models of the dancers.

Glass from Clay

The glass people actually began life as hunks of unformed clay. Sculptor Diana Walczak, co-founder of Kleiser-Walczak Construction Co., sculpted these hunks into near life-size models of human beings. She created them both with and without armor. To speed her work, she built only half of each model using a mirror down their middles to give her the full feeling of their symmetry. These clay figures were then cast in fiberglass and digitized into the computer. Once inside the computer, the single halves were reflected about their central axes to create the full figures.

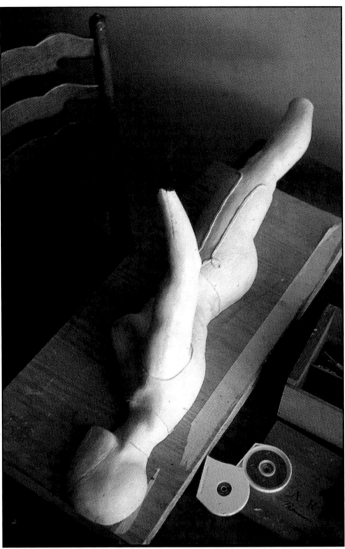

Sculpted in clay and then digitized into the computer, this half-body of a woman with armor served as the model for the female glass dancer.

Bringing Them to Life

Using the captured motion, Jeff Kleiser's team then attached the movements to Walczak's computer models. The motion was also attached to a series of flaming priests that appeared in the dream sequence as well as to spiral strands of DNA that come jutting out into the audience.

Throughout the process of animation, each of the animators involved worked in 3-D stereo. Normally, with flat images, all an animator has to be concerned with is getting the image in the right place on the film frame. With stereo imagery, however, it must not only be in the right place on-screen, but in the right spot in space as well. If they were even the slightest bit off, miss-registration of the imagery would cause the effect to fall apart.

The Final Look

Creating the final frames of the glass-people sequence was one of the most computer-intensive phases of the entire production. Not only did they have to compute each frame twice, once for each eye to produce the stereo effect, but they also had to create the feeling of solid glass bodies. This meant they had to use a form of what is called ray tracing, in which the paths of millions of separate light rays have to be followed as they pass through the dancers' bodies. Without this approach, neither the reflections nor the refractions of light around and through their bodies would have looked right. Fortunately, they had the three massively powerful PVS computers to help them complete the shots.

A utopian vision of the future, complete with digital fireworks from "The Theatre of Time." The flying vehicles are all computer generated, while the buildings and walkways below are miniatures shot on the Trumbull Company's motion-control stage.

The Future: "Theatre of Time"

The last of the three attractions is called the "Theatre of Time" and continues the story begun in the first two. Here, the audience travels into four possible futures with the evil Osiris. The first is a bombed out dead world. The second looks as if it is soon heading in the direction of the first. Its cities have been wrecked by violence and repression, and rebel ships are fighting madly with police and military cruisers. The third future is less bleak than the first two, but still shows the world as a repressive police state.

Attraction Three

Hungry for world domination, Osiris kidnaps Mac and Carina and takes them on a ride into four possible futures. Seeing one he likes, Osiris jumps out of the time machine, pulling Carina with him. Mac is left behind and watches helplessly as the world evolves from bad to worse. With the world changing before him, Mac's love for Carina helps him discover a way to change it back. Quickly, he takes control of the time machine and, once again, saves Carina. Osiris, however, is left in the degenerate world he created as, together, Mac and Carina chart a course that brings them and the current world to a utopian vision of the future.

The final future, the one that Mac and Carina eventually bring about, is a true utopia. There, the earth is green and well cared for. The buildings are sleek, and the transportation is airborne and totally non-polluting. There is no sign of repressive law enforcement, and hundreds of people can be seen moving about in the squares and streets of the utopian cities.

Making the Future

Each of these futures began as a model set on Trumbull's motion control stage. Actually, their lives began somewhat before this in the Trumbull Company Image Engineering Department. There, the designs and basic city models were roughed out on computer. Some of the buildings were also developed in greater detail and sent to a computer-controlled laser cutter. The laser then cut the building forms out of plastic, and these were assembled to create the live models.

A dystopian view of the future with flying garbage scows, military vehicles, and smoggy computer-generated atmospheric effects.

Unobtanium, the Unknown Material

At one point, Kramer's group was asked by Trumbull to come up with the visual appearance of a futuristic material that looked like nothing that exists today. He called this material "Unobtanium." Kramer's group rose to the challenge, using every trick in the book of animation. They tweaked the reflective values of their various texture maps, used several levels of transparency, along with reflection maps and virtually anything they could think of. In they end, they discovered the new material, one that looked and behaved differently depending on what kind of light was shined upon it, and one that had certainly never been seen in the current day and age.

The cityscape data and building designs created by the Trumbull artists were also sent over the local network to Kleiser-Walczak's "future" team, headed by Ed Kramer, which was busily creating spaceships, garbage scows, police vehicles, rebel fighters, and crowds of computer-generated extras to be used throughout the various episodes. The city data helped Kramer's team position the various flying ships exactly where they were supposed to be in the live-action model shots.

Making Them Fit

All the computer graphic ships had to fit closely with the motion-control models. This was done by using the same camera move captured by the motion-control system on the model set, and by duplicating the lighting of the models inside the computer. In the case of the lighting, however, Kramer's team didn't copy the live-action light design at all. They found it faster and more effective simply to use their own eye. If the computer element looked as if it fit into the scene, then in fact it did. No more precise method was needed.

A more complex task of creating a sense of depth to the grand vistas of the various futures, however, involved a bit more work than just eye-balling it. In the real world, as objects move farther away, they "fade into the distance." This is due to the effects of the atmosphere, as well as the presence of elements like mists, smoke, and clouds. To imitate these effects, Kramer's team created a series of atmospherics, as they are called, and then applied them to their computer graphic ships as they moved off in the distance.

Populating the Future

Despite the realism of the atmospherics or any other visual effect, there is always one problem with model shots that is difficult to eliminate. No matter how detailed and realistic the sets may be, they almost always appear stark and lifeless because there are never any people in them. With computer animation, however, this is changing.

Using a single, basic Synthespian model from the Kleiser-Walczak library, Kramer's team populated the future with almost 1,000 computer-generated actors. Because of the intense computing requirements of this process, no individual scene contained more than 200 people at any one time. In the "dystopian" (anti-utopian) reality, they are seen as a group of 200 goose-stepping soldiers, while in the utopian future, they are collections of normal people milling about, walking hand-in-hand, and cheering the evening's fireworks.

Variety Is the Spice of Life

Variety, unfortunately, is not yet the computer's strong suit. When the computer creates a duplicate of something, it is an exact duplicate. It was obvious to the future team, however, that not everyone in the future could or should look the same, nor could they walk or act the same either. To introduce variation into their synthetic actors, Kramer built six different outfits for them to wear. Some had long sleeves, some short, some had gloves, as well as different hair and skin tones. These variations were then paired with four separate physical movements that were captured with Kleiser-Walczak's motion capture system. One of the motions was a sort of shuffling movement used to simulate milling about, another was clapping hands, a third involved raising both hands in the air, and the forth was a simple walk cycle.

These movements were then scattered throughout the crowds so that no two people were doing the same thing next to each other. In addition, the various movement cycles were offset so that no two people did exactly the same thing at the same time. The overall effect was to turn an otherwise sterile setting into one teeming with life.

Bringing It All Together

The Luxor project represents computer graphics' most adventuresome step into nonstandard film production. Virtually every attraction either projected standard film at extremely high rates, required something like stereographic imagery, or used an extra-large film format. The Theatre of Time, for example, projected double-sized film frames on a 70-foot high by 35-foot wide movie screen at twice the speed of normal film.

Each of these different technologies increased the complexity of the work by several times. Taking these more difficult technologies into consideration, it was estimated that the number of animation minutes created for Luxor could be translated into almost 50 minutes of feature film animation. With figures like this, can a full-length computer-generated feature be far behind?

The Earth is green and well cared for, and people ride in clean airborne transports in one of the final visions of the utopian future in "The Theatre of Time."

Help, I'm "Stranded": Super Drink Box Saves the Day

The squeals and laughter of rambunctious children fill the air, as a class-room of animated drink boxes squirm in their chairs. A paper airplane glides in front of the class, passing before the movie screen hung against the chalkboard which shows lists of today's "good" and "bad" students. Numbers count down on the movie screen, and the title "Drink Boxes Today. Writing Paper Tomorrow" announces the film.

The film begins, casting shadows of the front row juice boxes on the screen at the front of the class.

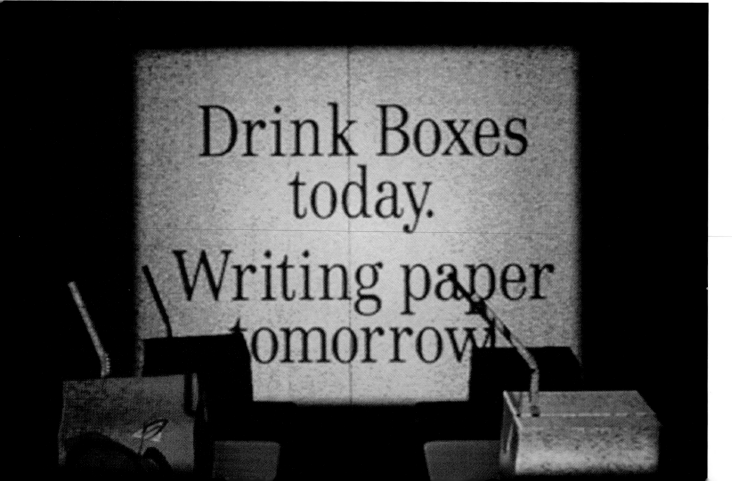

As the lights fall, the camera focuses on an apple juice box in the front row. He is bored and slowly falls asleep on his desk. The image wobbles and fades to his dream, where he is "Super Drink Box," flying across sunny skies with a paper cape trailing heroically behind him. Suddenly, he spies three lost drink boxes stranded on a desert island. A shark is circling ominously. In a flash of inspiration, the hero transforms himself into a piece of writing paper with the words "Help! We're Stranded!" written on it. Spying a passing recycling ship, he drops onboard, turns himself into a sail, and blows the ship to the island, saving the drink boxes.

The heroic dream slowly fades back to the classroom where a milk box is prodding the dreamer awake. The classroom film ends, and the drink boxes all hop up from their desks and into the recycling bin in front of the class. As they jump and tumble into the bin, the

© Pixar 1993

Still in the dark as the movie ends, the first two drink boxes jump into the recycling bin and bounce for joy. All of the 3-D objects shown here were already in Pixar's library and so had to be modeled for this advertisement.

movie screen rises to reveal in childish scrawl on the chalkboard behind them "The Drink Box Serves You Right."

© Pixar 1993

The juice box slowly falls asleep. Originally this shot was meant to be taken from a different angle; however the animators decided that this view communicated the action more clearly.

From Primitive to Sophisticated

Created by Pixar for Lintas:NY, this spot once again shows both Pixar's expertise in character animation, and the growing capability of the computer to create any look desired. In this case, the drink box commercial was designed to convey the

Super Drink Box spies the stranded juice boxes on the desert island. Behind him glows the red yarn sun in the yellow yarn sky.

feeling of the elementary school child's world. To that end, yarn art, construction paper cutouts, and primitive school-age drawing styles were employed, along with sophisticated 3-dimensional modeling and lighting techniques.

Creating animated life at Pixar always begins with a storyboard. Renowned for its evocative character animation, Pixar is often given free reign to create their commercial spots from scratch. In the case of the "Stranded" advertisement, Animation Director Roger Gould and Technical Director Oren Jacob took the initial set of storyboard ideas and reworked them with the client until the action evolved at the pace desired.

Animatic is a scene-by-scene video of the storyboard.

The lettering and the lines on this piece of computer-generated paper were created by hand and then scanned into the computer.

Once the storyboard was set, they created what is called an *animatic*. By videotaping each storyboard image for the number of seconds that each shot would be on-camera, Gould and Jacob were able to get a good approximation of the commercial's timings. From this they could determine which scenes worked and which were no longer necessary (either because they didn't move the story along well enough or because there wasn't enough time to include them).

From Story to Model

The first step in any computer graphics production involves modeling, the creation of the 3-D elements that will be used in the spot. Since "Stranded" was Pixar's second drink box commercial, and since their client wanted to use essentially the same beginning and ending as the first spot, virtually all the models of the boxes and the classroom had already been created. This meant that the desks, the drink boxes, the film screen, the chalkboard, the recycling bins, and more were in Pixar's digital libraries and had only to be brought out and re-animated. Thus, the only models that had to be built for this piece were the relatively simple 2-dimensional elements needed for the dream sequence.

Going Back to School

While most computer graphics modeling usually takes place on the computer, the animators at Pixar took a different tack with this commercial spot. To evoke the dream world of an elementary school child, animators Jeffrey Pidgeon and Rich Quade began their modeling task using a series of typical school supplies, including heavy construction paper and colored pencils. They physically cut the paper into the desired shapes and drew on these shapes with the colored pencils. As each shape was completed, it was scanned into the computer and used to create a computer graphic element for the animation.

For example, to create the ocean waves, two separate wave patterns were cut, drawn, and scanned into the computer, where their outlines were traced using a digital paint program. These outlines were subsequently used to create identically shaped, flat computer-graphic models that could be moved and animated inside the computer-generated dream environment. A similar approach was used to create the shark, the birds, and the desert island

The elements of this image were first created using construction paper, sandpaper, yarn, glue, and colored pencils. The resulting artwork was then scanned into the computer.

© Pixar 1993

Super Drink Box (as the paper cry for help) lands in the middle of the recycling ship. Only the boxes and the bin itself are 3-D objects; the rest of the elements are 2-dimensional.

Turning into a sail, the hero blows the ship to the island and saves the day. Note how the drink boxes are positioned to give a feeling of three dimensions to the flat island and palm tree.

© Pixar 1993

with its single palm tree. In the case of the island, however, its sandy texture was produced by cutting its shape from a rough grade of sandpaper instead of smooth construction paper.

Sunny Skies

The final element created for the dream sequence was the sky backdrop. The agency's original concept was to use paper and pencil for this as well, but creative director Pete Doctor had a different idea. He wanted something that would provide a greater sense of texture and warmth. To that end, the animation team explored several alternatives based on the various materials that kids use to create art in the classroom, looking at things such as elbow macaroni and glitter, before finally deciding on yarn.

Animator Quade then built a one-square-foot section of sky by painstakingly gluing pieces of yarn on paper, working outwards in a tight spiral starting at the center of the sun. Several different colored yarns were tested, before he finally settled on a vibrant combination of red and yellow. The final yarn painting was then scanned into the computer, where it served as the backdrop for the entire

dream sequence. Because of the precision of the scanner, the texture of the yarn was as visible on computer as it had been on paper.

Other Handiwork

In addition to the 2-dimensional cutouts used in the dream sequence, the Pixar animators also physically created the piece of paper into which the hero box transforms himself, along with the lettering on that paper. Despite the advances in computer font design, no print face could adequately capture the primitive and erratic

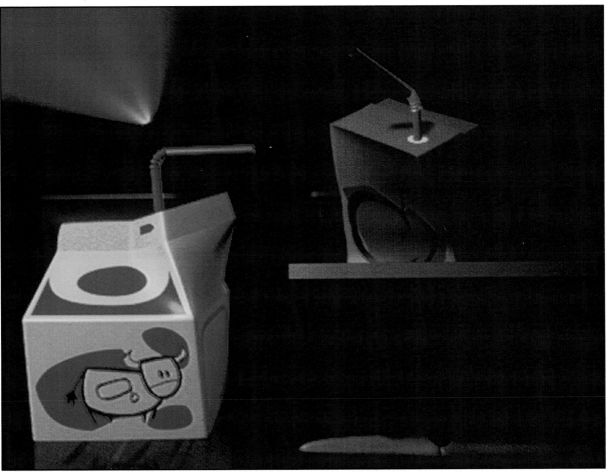

© Pixar 1993

The dream ends as the milk carton prods the juice box awake. Notice how the boxes and the desks are lightly illuminated by the movie light reflected from the film screen in front of them.

style of a child's hand-printed letters. Doing this task by hand gave the team greater control over the final look and also served to heighten the warmth and personality of the commercial spot.

Bringing Boxes to Life

After the new models for the dream sequence had been constructed and the existing models were dusted off and readied for action, it was time to begin the animation. Despite the fact that both the beginning and ending sections of the piece were essentially the same as in the first drink box commercial, animation director Gould wanted some different movements from the boxes in the classroom.

Since the shapes of the objects to be animated were extremely simple, this process was fairly straightforward.

They used various squash-and-stretch distortions to give extra bounce and a child's sense of enthusiasm to the irrepressible student boxes. In the course of re-animating the opening classroom scene, however, the animators discovered that the storyboard needed to be changed for the shot where the drink box begins to fall asleep.

Initially, it called for filming the drink box from behind as his head drifted downwards to the desk. Unfortunately, because of the camera angle, it was difficult to tell exactly what was happening, and so the camera position had to be moved. Changing camera angles in a live-action shoot can cause long delays and a great deal of extra expense. In the computer graphics world, however, it is merely a case of telling the camera to move to another location. The animators simply shot the action from a different position leaving the "acting," or animation, exactly as it was before.

Moving into Dreamtime

A recognizable vocabulary of special effects has been established in film and television to convey to the viewer that the action is now entering the dream world. It usually consists of things like slowly closing in on the actor's head, distorting the picture in some fashion, and changing the soundtrack to indicate that something different is happening. This same vocabulary was used for "Stranded." The music drops as the camera closes in on the wilting drink box. When his head touches the desk, the picture wavers and then fades into the start of the dream.

To produce the wobbling transition, Technical Director Jacob first created a 12-by-12 grid onto which the image of the dozing box was pasted. Animator Andrew Schmidt then used the intersections of this grid as his animation control points. Moving a point on the grid distorted the image near that point. By moving a succession of these points Schmidt was able to create a rippling distortion that could serve as the transition mechanism both into and out of the dream. In the process, he carefully avoided moving any of the grid points along the edges of the image. This would have caused the picture to pull away from the edge of the monitor or television screen and ruin its 3-dimensional feeling. Instead of looking like a distorted scene from a 3-dimensional reality, it would have seemed more like a rippling piece of paper with a picture pasted on top of it.

© Pixar 1993

Everyone is overjoyed by the rescue, except perhaps the shark. There are between 10 and 20 elements layered on top of each other to create this image. Note how the simulated shadows vary with each element and add to the feeling of depth.

Living the Dream

Once inside the dream world, the animation becomes a mix of 2- and 3-dimensional effects. The computer-scanned paper cutouts were placed one in front of the other to provide a kind of 2 $\frac{1}{2}$-dimensional feeling. With the look of an elementary school drama, the two lines of waves are slid back and forth in front of the background. The cutout shark with its hand-drawn, toothy grin, and the recycling bin sailboat move between the wave cutouts as the drama unfolds.

The primary challenge for the animators in this sequence lay in anchoring the 3-dimensional drink boxes to this 2-dimensional reality. For example, the boxes stranded on the desert island couldn't look as though they were just stuck onto the island's surface. By artfully squashing and tilting the boxes, as well as slouching one of them against the base of the palm tree, the effect succeeded. Not only did it support the 3-dimensional nature of the boxes, but it also heightened the scene's dream-like quality by accentuating the flatness of the surrounding environment.

Providing the Final Look

Since Pixar has pioneered much of what is called "rendering" (the creation of the final look of a computer graphic image), many of their pieces often include complex and subtle shadowing and lighting effects. For the "Stranded" spot, they needed to evoke both the feeling of being in a movie theater, and that of being inside a dream world.

Going to the Movies

For the movie theater effect, Pixar used artwork that was sent to them from their client. The artwork was first scanned into the computer, and then various scratches and film grain effects were added to it to imitate the feeling of seeing a well-used, educational film strip. It was then projected in black and white to further enhance its film-like nature.

To anchor the boxes inside the "movie theater" environment, they were shown both from behind, with the projector light casting shadows of their tops and straws onto the screen at the head of the class, and from in front, being lit by the reflected brightness coming off the screen. In addition, the lighting of the entire classroom environment changed over time just as the lighting does in a real movie theater when images of varying brightness are projected onto the screen.

Lost in the Dream

While the lighting and shadows of the classroom helped to accentuate that environment's reality, in the dream sequence, they served to heighten its topsy-turvy nature. The sun and sky are in the background throughout the sequence, yet all the shadows are cast from front to back. What's more, there are even shadows cast against the sky itself. This latter effect adds a playful note to the whole piece and gives viewers the feeling that they are watching an elementary school stage drama.

As is often the case, effects that look simple are often the hardest to create. In the case of the dream sequence, its primitive appearance hides a complex series of steps required to bring it about. First of all, none of the shadows are real in the sense that they were cast by shining a computer light on a computer-graphic object. They were all created by making duplicates of the objects themselves and then offsetting the object and its shadow.

For example, to provide the palm tree with a shadow, its 2-dimensional shape was first duplicated on the computer. Then the colors of the copy were altered, and a level of transparency was added to allow the background to show through it. Once the colors and transparency were set, the duplicate was attached to the original palm tree, but was given a small offset so that it wouldn't match the tree's position exactly.

The same approach was used for the water, the shark, and every other 2-dimensional element in the scene. The amount of offset or visible shadow depended upon how far away from the next layer the shadowed element was supposed to be. The birds have smaller amounts of visible shadow than the palm tree does because they are closer to the sky.

Layers upon Layers

The manner of shadowing mentioned above, while relatively easy to do, added a great deal of complexity to the final compositing stage. Instead of having to merely layer the main elements of front waves, shark, island, back waves, birds, and sky (in that order), the compositor now had to add shadow layers for each of these elements as well. In some cases, this meant keeping track of up to twenty separate layers of imagery. Depending on how the various objects were interacting, it was often difficult to keep all the layers in their proper order.

The film is over, and the lights are coming back up as the drink boxes cavort in the recycling bin. The shadows in this image were created by shining computer lights on the objects shown.

The Finishing Touches

Once the final images had been rendered and composited, the spot was ready for post production. Here the giggles and squeals of the excited drink boxes were added, along with the final voice track. The result was an immensely humorous spot, with a very timely message that both young and old could appreciate.

It is also interesting to note, though, that not all the humor of the piece was immediately apparent to the viewer. If you recall the opening scene of the commercial, it contained a small paper airplane that glided past the movie screen and two lists of the day's "good" and "bad" students. Below each of those words were listed the first names of the animators who participated in the spot. While the work of computer animation is often difficult and can require long hours, there is always room for a good sense of humor.

19

Perrier and the French Foreign Legion

The camera tilts down on a table top covered with tin soldiers in a toy collector's apartment. It is a sweltering summer day. The enemy is thirsty. Suddenly, a shrill whistle breaks the silence, and the toy soldiers spring to life. An all-out assault on the refrigerator is planned to save not only the soldiers but all the other toys in the house.

Alive and ready, the lead soldiers follow their leader. Note the sharp focus on the front soldier while those in the background are blurred. Computer cameras have variable focal-length lenses that behave just the way live-action cameras do.

Courtesy of Perrier Export

Two by two, they march across the tabletop. Sliding down the table's leg, they skirt past a shaggy dog and head for the kitchen. There, they blast open the refrigerator door and find it stocked to capacity with Perrier. One of the bottles falls on its side. The top blasts off from the shaking, and the cool, refreshing Perrier mineral water drenches the cheering crowd below.

The Digital World Is Everywhere

With the ease of modern telecommunications, it was a simple task for the French mineral water company, Perrier, to hire George Lucas' Industrial Light & Magic (ILM) to create a commercial for the European market. With ILM's expertise in computer graphics film effects, it was no problem for them to make the transition to a commercial production. Actually, ILM has a growing commercial presence and uses the more steady flow of commercial work to supplement their film production.

For effects supervisor Ken Ralston and computer graphic effects director Doug Smythe (both Oscar winners for their work on the film *Death Becomes Her*), the project looked like a perfect spot for some fairly straightforward computer animation. The soldiers had to be brought to life, but they were not to lose the look and feel of toys.

What About Puppets?

This sort of advertisement, where the action is animated but not human, is often ideally suited for puppetry. The benefits of puppetry are that you can see and judge the puppeteer's performance in real time, and there is no need to spend days or weeks modeling the elements. That time can be more productively used perfecting the live performance.

In the case of this ad, however, puppetry was immediately ruled out for all but a few of the other toys in the house. The number of soldiers (over 70) to be animated for the spot would have required coordinating such a large crowd of puppeteers that the only possible outcome was chaos. The computer's capability to duplicate models and to control their motions far outweighed any amount of spontaneity that might have come from a live performance.

In addition, computer graphics could deliver something puppetry could not, an easily refinable set of actions. If any part of the computer animation were not perfect, an animator could continue to work on that section until it was. With puppetry, if even one small part of the performance were off, the whole sequence would have been ruined. The puppeteers would then have had to start from the top with the possibility that something else could go wrong.

Courtesy of Perrier Export

Bicyclists climb the staircase. This was one of the few elements done with puppetry. ILM used rod puppets—models with metal rods attached to their movable parts—to animate this scene. The rods were later erased by the computer.

The soldiers march across the floor. Marching in unison is created by first working out a computer walk cycle, and then attaching it to each soldier. To march them in unison, each soldier begins and ends the cycle at the same time. For variety throughout the spot, the ILM animators changed the beginning of the walk cycle for each soldier. Note also the soldiers' shadows. These were created by the computer and then composited into the live action.

From Real World Models to Computer Graphics Elements

The first step in creating the Perrier toy soldiers was to construct a series of physical models in the ILM model shop. There, they built a 13-inch maquette and cast 70 three-inch tall soldiers. The larger model served as the primary visual reference for the animation team, while the smaller soldiers were used as props for the opening live-action scene.

After their stage performance, which consisted of standing still on a table top, the smaller soldiers were then given to the animators as further reference guides and as motivational aids. Mock battles sprang up regularly throughout the studio as animators waited for their renderings to complete. None of these physical models were digitized directly with a 3-D digitizer, because they determined that the hand-built approach would work better for them.

A 3-D digitizer is a device that can automatically create a computer graphics model from an existing physical object.

Following Orders

As the modeling moved forward, Ralston worked on the timing of each scene. This was particularly difficult for this spot since virtually all the action was being created on computer. To give himself and the animators a good feel for the pace of the action, he glued two rows of the soldiers onto a sheet of plastic and filmed it as it was dragged slowly across the tabletop. From this, the animators were able to create a one-second walk cycle that could then be applied to all of their computer graphic soldiers.

Besides providing a clear sense of the commercial's timing, the plastic strip of soldiers also helped anchor one particular effect in the live-action reality. Directly after the soldiers come to life, they march across the tabletop and pass behind a clear drinking glass full of water, which refracts and distorts their images. To create this shot, effects director Doug Smythe split the frame vertically along both the left and right edges of the glass. On either side he then composited the computer graphics soldiers. Behind the glass, however, he kept the footage of Ralston's toy maquettes that had been glued to the plastic sheet and slowly dragged across the tabletop. The distortions created by the water and glass made it impossible to see that the soldiers in back of the glass were not actually

Courtesy of Perrier Export

A close-up of the action. In creating these soldiers, the ILM animators wanted a hand-painted look. They used a digital paint system to smear the paint in various areas and to add scuffs to show how well the soldiers had been used.

the sliding soldiers were directly in contact with the table leg. To overcome this problem, the animation team built a precise computer model of the live-action table leg and then animated the soldiers with respect to that model. They could then test their animations by bringing up the live-action plate of the real table and laying their animation on top.

After sliding down the leg, the soldiers regrouped on the floor. Here, they were faced with a potentially dangerous foe, a shaggy dog. The dog, of course, was filmed in live action while his trainer put him through the paces. The key to the scene was to make the dog's eyes move as if he were seeing the soldiers. This was done by tying a doggy treat to a wire and moving it back and forth in front of his face. The wire and food were later painted out of the frames with ILM's digital paint system.

Canine Caper

Working with animals is never easy, no matter how well they are trained. In this case, however, they got more than they had bargained for. As the trainer hid under the table waving the treat in front of the dog, the dog became

moving their arms and legs. This trick saved the computer graphics team from having to model the glass and do the heavy calculations needed for accurate defractions.

Down the Table Leg

As the computer graphics soldiers reached the edge of the table, they then had to slide down the table leg to the floor below. The difficulty here was making sure that

Making Contact

Creating believable interactions between computer graphics and live action is difficult. In the case of the dog above, it was one of perseverance and plain old good luck. There are also several other ways that serve to anchor computer elements in the live footage; one of which is making sure that the graphics elements appear to contact the live-action props in a believable way.

In the Perrier spot, this meant that the soldiers' feet had to touch the tabletop and the floor when they marched, their bodies needed to hug the table leg as they slid to the floor, and their shadows had to fall on the objects around them.

To ensure contact, the ILM animators scanned the live-action plates into their computers and then laid their wireframe soldiers on top of it. With this view of the action, they could then tweak the placement of the soldiers until the contact looked just right.

For the soldiers' shadows, they created precise models of the tabletop, table leg, and floor. Computer lights matching the set lighting were shined on the soldiers and made to cast shadows onto these models. These shadows were then cut from the computer animation and pasted into the live action during the final composite.

irritated at not getting his reward. He then turned his head to the trainer and barked. Unwanted animal reactions usually ruin a scene, but this turned out to be a winner.

Since the trainer was under the table, it looked as if the dog's eye's were focused directly on the table leg when he barked. This gave Smythe's animators a chance to add another extra bit of character to the piece. Instead of just marching past the dog as it looked back and forth, several of the soldiers glanced fearfully up at him as he barked, worried that perhaps they might get eaten. This additional piece of interaction between the live action and the computer graphics served to reinforce the soldiers' sense of reality.

Getting a Feel for the Characters

Animators are actors who sit in chairs. Instead of using their bodies and voices, their tools of the trade are the keyboard and the mouse, or perhaps a custom control device. Just as with a stage actor, the major challenge for any animator is to get inside the character and see what makes it work.

To get inside the Perrier soldiers, Smythe's animators physically acted out their parts. They created paper toy-soldier hats and took over one of the ILM soundstages. The entire exercise was videotaped both to give them a sense of the timing needed and to help them see what kinds of movements looked right. These shots were then scanned into their computer workstations so they could refer to them as they animated.

Variety, the Spice of Life

Computer graphics is at its best when it comes to creating duplicates of existing computer models. Virtually any number can be created almost instantly. This feature was essential for creating the gallimimus dinosaur herds in *Jurassic Park* and was instrumental in creating the 70 soldiers for this Perrier spot. The

flip side of this coin, however, is that anything that is duplicated by computer is copied exactly. Variation does not come naturally.

To combat the tendency of the computer to slicken and homogenize the look of its creations, Smythe had his animators create several different paint jobs for the various soldiers. The paint jobs include misapplied blobs of color as well as metallic scrapes because he wanted the soldiers to look hand-painted and well-worn.

Besides varying the soldiers' looks, Smythe's group also made sure that none of the soldiers moved in precisely the same way. Although the soldiers' one-second walk cycle had been determined early on, it was not uniformly applied to every soldier. By introducing delays or shifts in movement, the potential lock-step look was completely avoided, thus enhancing each soldier's individuality.

The Final Step

After sliding down the table leg and slipping past the dog, the troops amass before the white expanse of the refrigerator door. The cannon fires, and the soldiers let out a victory cry of "We won!" as the refrigerator door blows open. A single bottle of cool Perrier falls over, pops its top, and drenches them all. As the spot closes, one soldier is on his knees with his arms spread, a couple of others have lost their hats, but they all are celebrating.

In this climactic final scene, only the soldiers are computer graphics. The rest was shot live-action including the blasting of the refrigerator door, which used the explosion created for the destruction of the death star in the film *The Empire Strikes Back*. To complete the spot, all that remained was to composite the various elements into the blank plates shot at the start of the project. The result was a 45-second commercial to be run in movie theaters all over France, and a 30-second piece for European television.

Victory at last! Perrier rains down upon them all. This mass of celebrating soldiers shows several of the variations in their paint jobs and uniforms. A sense of their individuality is also gained by the various reactions shown to the cool Perrier shower.

Courtesy of Perrier Export

20

Snow White Goes Digital

"Hi Ho, Hi Ho . . ." sing the seven, dusty dwarfs as they march mer-
rily off to work, tossing their picks and shovels onto their shoulders. Tipping their hats to the dusty and smudged Snow White,
they leave their dirty little home in the hazy woods. . . .

The dwarfs have cleaned up their act. Note the sharp focus, the clear border, and the much more believable skin tones,
which have lost their rosy-orange overcast.

Snow White talks to the dwarfs (before digital cleaning). Note the heavy, bluish tones overall and the red discolorations to the left of Doc's hat.

© The Walt Disney Company

Wait a minute, something's wrong. Is Snow White, the image of ultimate purity, not really as scrubbed and spanking clean as her name implies? If truth be told, that was the case until just recently. In 1992, she was 55 years old and in bad need of a face-lift and a good cleaning. Disney, which started an ambitious restoration of its film archive five years earlier, had not yet returned her to her former glory because they were searching for a restoration technique worthy of her perfection.

The First Animated Feature

And understandably so, for *Snow White* was the cornerstone of the current multi-billion dollar Disney empire. It was the very first feature length animation ever created and the first animated film to win an Oscar. Before attempting *Snow White*, the longest Disney film was slightly less than seven minutes.

The project began in 1934 when Disney, one evening, announced to his studio personnel that they were going to attempt the impossible. He then spent the next four hours in a dramatic retelling of the Grimm Brothers' story of Snow White, which, by the time he'd finished, had won everyone over to the project. These beginning

four hours stretched to three years before the film was complete. By that time, over 750 people had worked on the feature, and its costs had soared to 10 times the original budget of $150,000.

Despite money shortages and severe technical challenges, the film was completed and released in 1937. Within three months, nearly 20 million people saw it, breaking all previous box office records. To date, after eight re-releases, *Snow White* has earned Disney Studios over $300 million, most of it at the 25- and 50-cent admission prices of past decades. When these figures are translated into today's dollars, its earnings come to well over a billion dollars.

Cleaning Up Snow White's Act

With such a lucrative property, it is little wonder that Disney wanted the best for *Snow White*. In the course of its five decades of life, the film had already gone through several different restorations, including creating new master prints, and actually washing and reusing the celluloid itself. Each restoration improved the film's quality somewhat, but also introduced extra defects, such as scuffs, scratches, and dust.

In fact, dust was the biggest problem of all. A perfectly clean film environment is impossible to find, and minute particles of dust had gotten sandwiched in between the glass plates used to hold the individual animation cels during photography. In addition, the cels themselves also created problems. Each animation drawing, or cel, is made up of several layers of acetate on which separate line art and colors are drawn. When layered together they create the full-colored frame. Occasionally, however, the layers did not go together as precisely as they should have and so the edges of the characters were fuzzy.

Disney wanted to remedy all of these problems without damaging the look and feel of the original film. The real difficulty lay in the fact that many of the problems, such as the dust and the fuzzy edges, were photographed into the film. Thus, any restoration process that merely created a new film copy would not be able to eliminate them. What was needed was a method that could disassemble the animation image by image, correct the various defects, and then rebuild the film in its original form.

Digital to the Rescue

The prince charming whose kiss would bring Snow White back to life was computer graphics. Disney had already used digital video technology to restore and enhance the video release of *Fantasia*, and so they were aware of its potential. But working in film, with its vastly increased resolution, was another proposition entirely. Until the early 1990s, no system existed that could handle the almost unimaginable quantities of digital data in a timely fashion to make it feasible.

A single frame of film requires about 40 megabytes (40 million bytes) of data to capture all its detail and range of color. An average film has over 130,000 such frames bringing the total amount of data to almost five

© The Walt Disney Company

It is hard to believe that this is even from the same film, let alone that it is the same frame as above. The colors have been restored to their original intensities, and the film defects have been entirely removed.

Once again, the blue cast overwhelms the image's colors. There is also heavy scuffing that has damaged the frame itself.

terabytes, or five trillion digital bytes. To provide a little perspective on how much data this is, five terabytes would fill 25,000 personal computer disks of 200 megabytes each. On top of this, there are the difficulties associated with scanning that number of frames into the computer and later printing them all back out onto film.

Kodak Cinesite

Kodak, the world's leading producer of film stock for the motion picture industry, was keenly aware of these problems. They were also aware that digital technology was quickly moving into the filmmaking business, and realized that unless they moved in that direction, too, much of their business might be lost. They saw that in the not-too-distant future virtually all the intermediary steps of filmmaking, from just after the film was shot to just before the final print was made, would be done with computer graphics technology.

To help develop this emerging field, Kodak developed the Cineon system, which consists of a high-resolution film scanner for inputting the film, software, and hardware to manipulate the images in digital form, and a laser-based film recorder for output. With the system just out of the prototype stage, Kodak opened Cinesite, the world's first fully digital post-production house, in 1992. Disney was intrigued at its restoration potential, and so commissioned a 2,000 frame test on a section of *Snow White* to see if it might be possible to do the whole film in this fashion.

Eighteen Weeks, Flat Out

Ed Jones, president of Cinesite, completed the test successfully, and after a period of intense negotiations, won the job. Now the real work began. The Cinesite crew, headed by Jones and creative director Bruno George, were faced with scanning, restoring, and printing out a whopping 119,500 frames of animation in only 18 weeks. On top of this, the work had to be done on a system that, while it had been used for short sequences, was largely untested.

Scanning began immediately. Kodak's new CCD scanner was able to completely digitize an entire frame at the unheard of speed of one per every three seconds. Once in digital form, the frame was then sent to the network of digital workstations. The network consisted of 14 of the fastest Silicon Graphics image computers available at the time, that were kept busy 'round the clock. Throughout the project, Cinesite ran three eight-hour shifts and employed over 60 people. Interestingly enough, not all the digital painters and "Dust Busters" were artists or even in the film business. Because their system was so easy to use, they were able to hire across the board, bringing on secretaries, receptionists, stockbrokers, and more.

Breaking It Down

To get a handle on the workload, Jones and George, in close collaboration with Disney, first broke the film down into average shots of 170 frames each. These shots were then brought up frame by frame on the workstations where the artists would begin to remove the dirt and paint out other visual distortions such as scrapes, scuffs, or unwanted highlights. The first difficulty they encountered when they began to correct the frames was learning to compensate for the differences between film and video imagery.

They discovered that some defects that were visible on the video screen did not show up when projected on a film screen, and vice versa. This was due to the very dif-ferent technologies used to create film and video images. At first, this caused some of the digital painters to paint too much or remove more dirt than there actually was. The hard part was that the image would look perfect on the monitor, but when it was projected in daily tests, the overcorrection would flatten or disrupt the grain of the film.

Scouring It Clean

The software Kodak developed allowed the image being worked on to be stripped down to its most elementary components. Using this system, a digital painter could isolate any element in the frame and then break it down into its three basic colors of red, green, or blue. Defects such as scratches or scuff marks could then be painted out. Dust or dirt that appeared on any of these layers could also be digitally washed away.

From image-processing research Kodak had completed in previous years, a series of computer programs (steps that tell a computer what to do) for automatic dust removal had already been developed. Coupled with an advanced digital-painting system developed by Pixar, these formed the heart of the Cinesite restoration system and allowed the technicians to wipe away most of the dust automatically and then retouch the image beneath. Unfortunately,

The Cineon system allowed Disney not only to remove the dust and discoloration from years of use, but also to eliminate the signs of any physical damage to the film stock itself.

The dusty dwarfs are smitten with love for Snow White. Heavy, blue flaring mars the upper left border of this frame, and the image is somewhat fuzzy.

the algorithms did not anticipate the complexities of working with all the various film technologies that had been used to create the current print of *Snow White*.

> Pixar is a computer animation house in northern California that is currently working on what will be the first entirely computer-generated feature film. The release date is 1995.

Each successive restoration of the film had added a new twist to the imagery. In order to disassemble the various color layers to get at the dust and defects, they first had to understand how these different twists had been introduced. This greatly slowed the project's initial progress, limiting their production of finished film frames to a few hundred a day. Once they got a good handle on the problem, however, everything moved much more smoothly so that by the end of the project, they were producing the system's daily capacity of 3,000 frames.

Putting It Back Together

In many respects, the *Snow White* cleanup was also a philosophical exercise. Film technologies have come a long way since 1937, and it would have been possible to create a much brighter and thoroughly modern version of *Snow White* had they wanted to. Fortunately, Disney and the Cinesite personnel involved in the project remained adamantly opposed to this. The goal from the start was not to create a brand new Aladdin-like version, but to re-create as closely as possible the film's original experience.

For many of the people involved, seeing *Snow White* in their childhoods had made such an impression on them that they wanted to be able to preserve that experience for generations to come. So, great pains were taken to rebuild the images in the exact form of the original. Disney even went so far as to bring in four of the original Snow White animators who were still alive. These animators, along with Disney vice-chairman Roy Disney, previewed the restored footage and made color recommendations based on their memories of the original work.

The dwarfs have cleaned up their act. Note the sharp focus, the clear border, and the much more believable skin tones, which have lost their rosy-orange overcast.

Winning by a Nose

The *Snow White* restoration project marked a first in the use of digital technology in film. Never before had every frame of an entire film been converted to digital imagery, manipulated in some way, and then printed back out to film. Its resounding success assures that it won't be the last.

During its execution, however, its successful completion was by no means a sure thing. While there was very close and open co-management of the project by Disney and Cinesite, Disney came very close on several occasions to closing it down. Progress at the beginning was disappointingly slow, on top of which not one of the interim deadlines was met. This made Disney Studios question whether the technology was actually as good as it had looked in the tests. In the end, however, they decided to stick with it and the restoration hit the final deadline right on the nose.

The finished film was delivered on special Kodak intermediate film stock from which new masters could be made. Along with the film came a truckload of digital tape containing all the corrected files for Disney's archives. Restored to its former splendor, the remastered *Snow White* was released once again in 1993, to a new set of children eager to share its magic. And it looks as if, with this application of digital-image technology, Snow White will truly live happily ever after.

21

Presto! A Talking Cat

In 1992, Disney needed a talking cat for its upcoming Halloween film, *Hocus Pocus*, a hilarious comedy about three 17th century Salem witches (led by Bette Midler) who are accidentally conjured into the present by an unsuspecting group of kids. Talking animals were nothing new; after all, "Mr. Ed" (the mischievous talking horse) and "Morris" (the overly finicky cat) had been around for a long time. All the same, Disney realized that with the ever increasing sophistication of film audiences, the standard trained-animal shots would not be believable enough. Nor was it likely that the often-used trick of placing peanut butter on the animal's upper palette would convince the audience that the animal was talking. The film required too many close-up shots for this technique to work.

Lip synching the digital cat required a lengthy process of trial and error. Here, the cat is both opening its eyes and speaking.

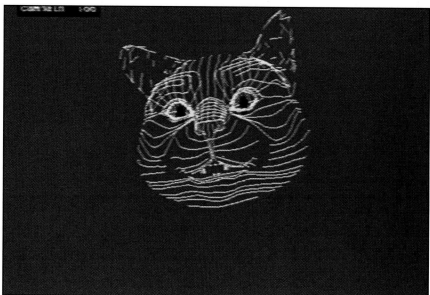

© The Walt Disney Company

Building an entire digital cat would have been impossible in the time available. However, creating just the head could be managed. Here we see the 3-D wireframe cat head element that Rhythm & Hues built and animated.

could easily stretch the cat's mouth open and closed making it look as if it were talking. Unfortunately, morphing's primary strength is also its major weakness. Since it only works in two dimensions, if the cat were to turn its head, its mouth would skew instead of moving smoothly into a profile. In addition, morphing gave the animators little control of other facial features, such as the eyes and tongue.

Morphing is the process by which the computer can smoothly and automatically transform one image into another.

This realization led executive producer Ralph Winter to consider two high-tech solutions to the problem: computer graphics and animatronic robots. He chose to pursue both avenues at the same time, building the robot as an insurance policy against the possible failure of the computer graphics approach. The cat robot, when it was completed, was constructed in a sitting position and could roll its shoulders, move its tail, head, and ears, and blink its eyes. Yet despite its relative level of sophistication, it was never used, because the computer graphics proved to be far more versatile.

Building a Digital Cat

For the computer graphics, Winter approached Bert Terreri, effects director at Rhythm & Hues, asking him to send all their available animal effects shot for review. Fortunately, they had just completed a commercial spot for Miller Brewery featuring talking chimpanzees, as well as another piece that included a talking pig. Terreri sent these to Disney for Winter's review, and the two of them began to discuss possible ways to create the desired effect.

To Morph or Not to Morph . . .

They decided that there were two primary approaches to consider. One was to animate a 3-dimensional computer graphics cat, and the other was to manipulate the cat's 2-dimensional picture image through morphing. At first, morphing appeared very promising. It was simple, easy to use, and would be very quick. With morphing, they

The Whole Cat . . .? No Way!

Because of these shortcomings, they began to explore 3-D graphics. At first, Disney wanted Rhythm & Hues to create a fully-animated computer graphics cat from head to tail. While this might be possible, given enough time and money, Terreri knew this was clearly not something to be attempted on a four-month film production schedule. He did think, however, that they could animate the cat's head and face within that time, and so agreed to a six-week test of their approach. If it proved successful, they would later re-attach the computer-animated head to the live-action body of the cat for the final film print.

Sculpting the Head

The first step in the process was to build an accurate, 3-D model of the cat's head. To get the necessary data, Terreri needed either to measure the cat's head and face dimensions physically, or to have the animal scanned by a laser scanner. The laser was ruled out because the cat would have to be put to sleep during the scan. This, in turn, would cause all its muscles to relax, resulting in a model that looked asleep rather than awake and alert. Instead, Terreri brought a sculptor to the film studio, and with calipers in hand, they carefully measured the placement and sizes of the eyes, eyebrows, mouth, nose, and ears of one of the six cats that was to star in the live action. Afterwards, the sculptor used that information to create a clay model of the head.

Digitizing the Sculpture

Once complete, the maquette was covered with a fine grid of lines and digitized to create a wire-frame model of the cat's skull. Terreri also scanned some existing film of the cat into the computer and cut the image of its head out of one of the frames. After the eyes were removed so Rhythm & Hues could insert its own 3-D eyeballs into the head's eye sockets, this cat image was then shrink-wrapped onto the computer-generated cat skull. The animators then brought it to life, moving its head, opening and closing its mouth, and rolling its eyes. Just to be sure the viewers wouldn't think Terreri had simply videotaped a very smart cat, he told his animators to wiggle one of the cat's ears as if it were waving to the audience.

It's All Yours

The test clinched the deal, and upon getting the job, Terreri immediately set up two groups at Rhythm & Hues: one technical and one animation. The animators were responsible for making the cat look and act real. They had to create and animate the head, make it talk, connect it to a computer-generated neck, and then attach the neck to the live-action body.

The technical people had to make sure that the software tools the animators needed were readily available. They wrote code to add control points to the wire-frame skull and then connected each point to the animation software. This allowed the animators to easily distort or move any part of the skull they pleased. In addition, since no facial feature moves in a vacuum, a program was developed to push and pull neighboring plates of the face whenever a control point was moved. Thus, if an eye winked, the eyebrow would be pulled down automatically and the cheek up, making the whole movement more believable.

Since the cat's skull had already been developed during the test phase, the animators had only to add 3-D models of both the tongue and the teeth to complete it. These were designed to slip inside the cat's skull like dentures and then anchor to a series of registration points inside the mouth cavity. They knew that a key element in creating the cat's character would be in how it exposed its teeth and tongue as it talked. They also knew that they could not rely on the live-action cat to provide the correct movements.

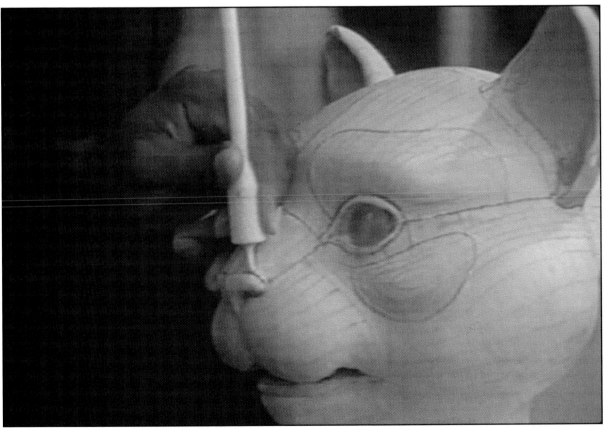

A lifelike sculpture of a cat's head, using measurements taken from one of the cats to be used for the film, was created and digitized to build the needed computer model.

Shooting the Live Action

At the same time that the modeling was taking place, the live-action footage was being shot. With the director's approval, Terreri had created a second-unit crew to help speed the cat shots. After the first unit had finished shooting the primary action, which usually included only one take of each animal scene, Terreri and the animal trainers would begin. Using stand-ins for the actors, he would shoot the additional takes to make sure the timings were right for the cat's dialog. If the cat did not stay in place the required amount of time in the primary shot, it could be cut from the second-unit's footage and composited into the final film.

depending on how close it was to the camera. To scale the computer graphics head properly, Terreri had to take precise measurements from the live-action set. His animators needed to know both the focal length of the camera lens, and how far the cat was from the camera during the shot. Given this information, the computer then automatically scaled the computer graphics head to the right size and placed it in the desired location.

Matching Without Motion Control

With the head in place for the starting frame of a shot, the animators then manually matched the movement of the real cat's head, frame by frame, throughout the rest of the sequence. Since the computer model was in wire frame, it meant that the animators could see through it to the film image beneath. Then, once the head motion was correctly matched, feature animation could begin. The first step was to take a sample map of the actual cat's face from the live-action film. Here, the lighting on the selected cat face had to match the lighting of the shot being animated; and the selected face had to be a frontal view in order to attach it properly to the computer graphics model.

© The Walt Disney Company

Here the digital cat head has been properly placed, or match-moved, with the live-action footage. It is now time to animate the expressions. Note the higher line densities around the eyes, ears, and mouth. This allows smoother, more subtle movements in these areas of the face.

Since cats tend to move their heads abruptly, finding an unblurred, full-faced shot with the right lighting was no easy task. Even when it could be located, it still did not guarantee success. Six cats were used

Both the first and second unit footage of the cat was then scanned into the computers at Rhythm & Hues to provide placement information for the animation. The first task was to match the movements of the computer-generated cat head with those of the real cat. But before this could take place, the size of the computer cat's head had to match the size of the cat's head in the live action. Even though the computer cat's dimensions were identical to the real cat, the apparent size of the real cat varied

to shoot the live action, and although they were all jet black, their facial structures varied slightly. When the animators mapped the chosen face onto the computer skull, it didn't always fit. Either the eye holes did not sit properly over the sockets, or the nose and mouth were slightly askew. When this happened, the underlying skull had to be gradually reshaped until the facial surface slipped into place. Then the eyes, teeth, and tongue could be inserted into the model.

Lip synching the digital cat required a lengthy process of trial and error. Here, the cat is both opening its eyes and speaking. Note the size of the cat's fangs. Disney producers had Rhythm & Hues greatly reduce the size of these digital teeth from those of a real cat so they wouldn't unnecessarily draw the viewer's attention.

© The Walt Disney Company

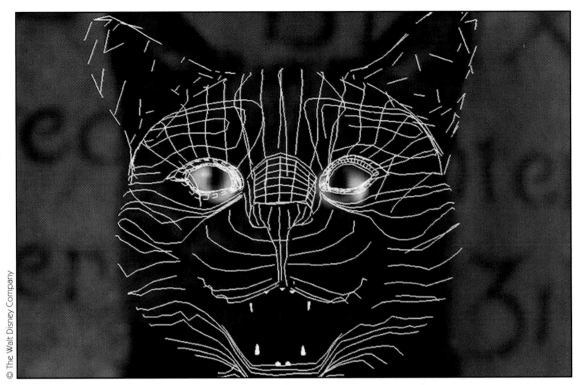

Can Cats Lip Synch?

Once the basic parts of the head had been assembled, it was time to synchronize the visuals to the voice track and begin animating the mouth. Over the more than 60 years that 2-D animation had been in existence, speech for that art form had been distilled to a basic set of eighteen mouth movements. Unfortunately for the Rhythm & Hues animators, these movements could not be easily translated to the 3-dimensional world of computer graphics. Nor did they find that direct imitation of human lip motion helped much. For example, making the cat round its lips for the sound of the letter "O" made it look extremely comical, destroying its believability. The animators at Rhythm & Hues were largely on their own and had to discover what looked right through a lengthy process of trial and error.

Completing the mouth animation marked the end of the first and most difficult stage of each of the more than 40 effects sequences. When a shot reached this point, it was time to go to the executive producer and director for approval of the animation. Keep in mind, however, that the computer graphics cat's head had yet to be connected to a neck and reattached to its body. For the animation approval, it floated in space above the cat's body and its invisible neck. Terreri did not want his animators or technical people to spend their time creating the neck until all the head movements had been approved. If they had done so and the director had then decided he wanted the cat to look in a different direction, then all the neck work would have been wasted.

Connect Head to Body, and You're Done

After approval, however, the neck could then be locked into place. Its primary challenge was to provide a believable support for the action of the head. Here the animators once again created a wireframe structure to which a surface could be attached. The technical people then sampled surface maps from various parts of the cat's body and stuck them onto the structure. Where the computer graphics neck met the live-action body, they used the technique of morphing to smooth the edge of one image into the other.

Once this process was complete, the shot was then sent to the film recorder, and the next sequence in the list was created. The more than forty effects shots required almost five months of dedicated effort by the animators, programmers, and directors at Rhythm & Hues. Yet, perhaps the most amazing aspect of it all is that this prodigious effort produced less than three minutes of computer animation.

22

The Temptation of a Lifetime: Death Becomes Her

Madeline teeters on the top step of the sweeping staircase. Ernest, her milquetoast husband, finally takes his destiny into his own hands and gives her the tiniest of nudges. Down she goes, head over heels, neck crunching, landing in a twisted jumble on the floor below as dead as she can be.

Meryl Streep, in the process of having her neck electronically twisted around backward.

As if this might happen everyday, Madeline (Meryl Streep) sits on the piano bench with her head on backward. Note the reflection in the mirror. Throughout the entire scene, her reversed reflection was visible here, involving some very fancy compositing.

Youth Obsession

The 1993 Universal Studios film, *Death Becomes Her*, is a comedy about the dark side of our culture's obsession with youth. Confronted by aging bodies and waning talent, two women succumb to the lure of eternal life. One small sip of a magic potion and they will live forever in the prime of life. With the promise of eternity, there are few who might choose otherwise. But, like any Faustian temptation, there are hidden consequences.

The panicked Ernest runs to call Helen, his lover. As he frantically tells her what has just happened, the jumble of limbs in the background begins to rise. Slowly, jerkily, Madeline lifts herself, dazed at what happened and becoming aware that something is horribly wrong. Her head is completely twisted around on a thoroughly broken neck. After a few false starts she backs towards Ernest, face first, to confront him with what he has done.

For Madeline and Helen, the consequences are that their bodies will go on living no matter what levels of mutilation and destruction they endure. And they endure a lot, what with broken necks, smashed heads, and shotgunned abdomens. Fortunately, they always have Ernest, Madeline's wimpy plastic surgeon husband, who through drunken dissolution has fallen from fame to undertaking. He is their ticket to beauty repair, and they are determined to make him immortal like themselves.

After the action was filmed, the entire scene was shot without actors to give the ILM's effects team what is called a clean plate.

© Ms. Streep had to act the entire scene backward, wearing a blue lycra cap to hold her hair and to later aid in digitally removing it.

Fiction, but Not Science Fiction

Until recently, the most spectacular computer graphics effects have been reserved for science fiction films. These films require pictures of aliens, prehistoric creatures, or nonearth environments that are difficult to create in any other way. As computer graphics has matured, however, it has made its way into other film genres, in this case the fantasy/reality mix of *Death Becomes Her*.

Although the digital effects required by this film were not the high-profile attention grabbers of a *Terminator 2* or a *Jurassic Park*, they did present some very difficult challenges, and their perfect execution won the effects team at Industrial Light & Magic (ILM) an Oscar. The primary difficulty for the most complex scenes lay in matching the created imagery to the human actors.

In virtually all of ILM's previous films, their computer imagery either started with a human and ended with an alien creature, or vice versa. They had never had to start with a real human, go through a series of believable changes, and then end up with a human again. This increases the difficulty of any digital effect immensely because of the subtlety of human motion. Viewers are accustomed to seeing human bodies move in certain ways. If an effect steps outside these expectations, it is spotted immediately, and the believability is ruined. For this reason, great care had to be exercised to get everything just right for this film.

The Regreening of Madeline

Madeline Ashton (Meryl Streep), former stage and screen star, is aging and she knows it. Her career is declining, and even her young lover is two-timing her. In desperation, she drives to the castle mansion of Countess Lisle Von Rhuman for her secrets of eternal youth and beauty. There, Madeline is presented with a vial of magic potion, which floats and glows and magically hovers on its pinpoint end.

After seeing the effects of a single demonstration drop daubed on her aging hands, Madeline quickly makes a deal with the countess and swallows the rest. She then watches in a mirror as her face and body transform before her eyes.

Floating Potion

For Computer Graphics Supervisor, Doug Smythe, these early scenes involved both digital painting and morphing. The mysterious egg-shaped vial of magic potion actually rested on a series of four prongs. In much the same way as described in the earlier section on wire removal, these

To capture Ms. Streep's head for the backward scene, she was filmed against blue screen while wearing a blue body suit. During this sequence she was filmed by two cameras, one for the frontal view and one for the profile to be stripped into the piano's mirror.

four prongs were painted out of each frame in which they appeared. The result was an otherworldly effect that enhanced the believability of the potion's magic.

Reverse Aging

With the audience and Madeline convinced of the potion's powers, Madeline swallows the liquid, and her transformation begins. To reverse the aging process, actress Streep was filmed in front of the mirror both with and without her age makeup. These shots were then scanned into the computer, and a computer morph between the two images was created. Morphing is the process by which one picture can be smoothly transformed into another by the computer.

Normally, creating a morph requires isolating the element being morphed by shooting it against blue screen with a motion-control camera. The blue screen can then be removed leaving only the element, ready for transformation and compositing into a clean plate. The motion control is necessary to match the blue screen shot to the camera move used to create the clean plate of the empty set.

None of this procedure, however, was necessary with Streep. Because of her remarkable acting abilities, she was able to match her physical movements during each shot almost exactly. This saved the effects crew a great deal of time in getting the final takes, and although there were slight differences in her hair, skin-tone, and lighting between the shots, they were not enough to affect the shot's believability.

Have a Nice Trip!

With a tap of his finger, Ernest (Bruce Willis) sends Madeline and her new body plunging to her death, or so we think. Fortunately for Madeline, this scene happens after she has drunk the magic potion that has immunized her to life's end. She is not, however, immune to its injuries. Her neck is broken, and her head is twisted 180 degrees as a result of the fall.

The execution of this remarkable effect involved the use of rod puppets, motion-control cameras, blue screen shots, and digital imagery and compositing. Manipulated by five puppeteers positioned beneath the stage floor, the broken Madeline slowly climbs to her feet and makes a few halting, confused steps towards Ernest who is talking frantically on the telephone. As the frightened Ernest tells Helen (Goldie Hawn) what has happened, his elbow

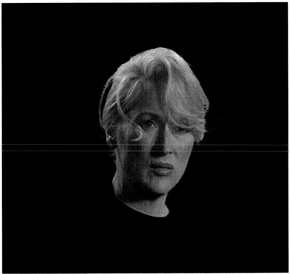

Here, Ms. Streep's head has been digitally extracted and will now be attached to her body at the piano.

To complete the elements needed, a ponytail was filmed against blue screen. In the lower corner of the image is a TV monitor with the scene playing. The effects technician is watching the action to determine how to move the ponytail.

momentarily obscures the puppet, and from that point on in the film, live-action footage of actress Streep replaces the puppet.

Acting Backward

To make Madeline's body orientation believable, Streep had to act this entire scene backward. What's more, she had to act it with a tight blue lycra baggy covering her head. The blue baggy was used to hold in her hair so it wouldn't obscure her neck and shoulders, and to later guide the removal and replacement of her head.

The scene was shot by hand-directed motion-control cameras that recorded the camera's movements automatically. This allowed Smythe's team to immediately shoot a duplicate clean plate of the same set, using an identical camera move without the actors present. From this clean plate, Smythe's group then extracted the parts of the image that were hidden by Streep's baggy-covered head. Once these elements were composited over the live-action shot, it looked as if her head were completely gone.

Bringing Back the Head

To capture Streep's real head so they could put it on her body the wrong way, they then shot her against blue screen. She was dressed in a full body suit of blue with only her head exposed. Sitting in a rotating chair, she was then filmed speaking her lines, and the chair was turned at the appropriate times to simulate her turning her head from one side to the other as she walked.

This was all filmed using the same motion-control camera move recorded from the live action pass to ensure that when the elements were composited together they would fit. At the same time as she was filmed in the chair, a set of computer-controlled dimmers, a large ring of surrounding lights, simulated the lighting environment of her pass through the live-action set.

The Final Twist

The end of the scene shows Madeline sitting at the piano in the living room. A profile view of her backward head shows in the mirror placed on the piano top. In frustration and anger at her predicament, she finally takes matters into her own hands and wrenches her head back the way it belongs. Meanwhile, still in the rotating chair, actress Streep grabs her real head, grimaces, and the two strong stagehands holding her chair spin it violently around 180 degrees. Then slowly, they turn the chair back again as she groans with relief and faces the camera.

To create this final realignment, Streep was shot from two sides against blue screen as her chair was spun by the stagehands. Two camera angles were needed in order to extract the view of her head the audience sees from the primary camera as well as the profile view in the mirror. Once again, Streep's blue-baggy head was removed using a clean plate, and the two views of her head were composited onto her body and into the piano mirror.

Creating the Neck

Throughout this scene, Madeline's neck has been twisted around like a piece of rubber. Its grooves and wrinkles swirl like the stripes on a barber pole. As real as this neck appeared, it was pure computer graphics from start to finish. Though initially built as a physical prosthetic device, it had to be reconstructed in computer imagery because Streep's skin was too sensitive to the materials of the prosthetic itself.

To build the computer neck model, the physical device was first scanned using a laser scanner. This created a computer structure that, unfortunately, didn't offer the precise controls Smythe's animators required. Instead, it was used as a guide for creating a second computer model that better served their needs.

Once the neck was finished, its skin was colored and textured to match Streep's own skin tone. The final task was to animate its movements to match the movements of Streep's head. The animators not only had to deal with its final dramatic untwisting, but also had to introduce various bobs and shifts to make sure it looked as if it were bearing the head's weight. After the animation was complete, the neck was composited in place.

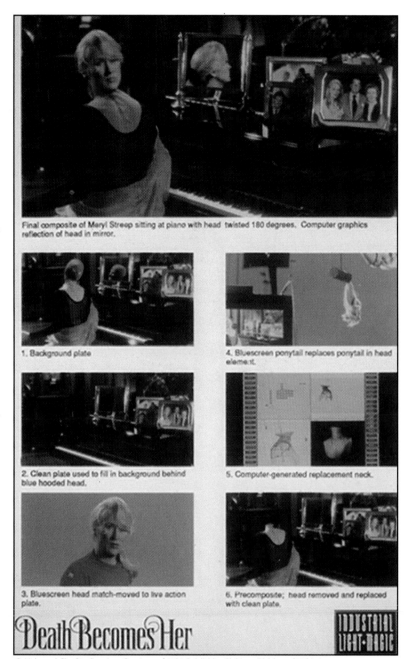

Final composite of Meryl Streep sitting at piano with head twisted 180 degrees. Computer graphics reflection of head in mirror.

1. Background plate

2. Clean plate used to fill in background behind blue hooded head.

3. Bluescreen head match-moved to live action plate.

4. Bluescreen ponytail replaces ponytail in head element.

5. Computer-generated replacement neck.

6. Precomposite; head removed and replaced with clean plate.

Death Becomes Her

INDUSTRIAL LIGHT + MAGIC

All together now! This slide shows the various steps from the clean plate to the final frame. Note both the lower right where Ms. Streep's head is completely missing, and the digital model for the neck replacement.

Blow Me Down!

As if Madeline's neck problems weren't enough trouble, her long-standing feud with Helen (Goldie Hawn) finally reaches a peak. She discovers that Helen is trying to steal back Ernest (Bruce Willis), whom Madeline had stolen from Helen almost two decades earlier. Determined to finish her rival for good, Madeline confronts Helen in the living room, shoves a double-barreled shotgun into her stomach, and pulls the trigger.

The resulting blast marks the beginning of the second major effects sequence in the film, which used exploding dummies, live-action stunt work, animatronic puppets and a 2-dimensional digital image manipulation technique to create a massive hole through Hawn's body. For the gun blast, a dummy likeness of Hawn, with a pyrotechnic charge in its belly, blasts apart sending bits of innards out its back. This shot was then intercut with a live action scene of Hawn's stunt double being yanked 30-feet backward through the air on a wire harness.

Helen's body ends up in the fountain outside, presumably dead. But, she too has taken a swig of the countess' potion. Slowly, her body stands up from the water to reveal a massive hole blown straight through her, out of which buckets of blood-tinged water is now draining.

Like Madeline's resurrection, this was an animatronic puppet. In this case, however, the robot was headless so a dump-tank of water could be drained through its neck and out the body hole as it stood up. Hawn's head was subsequently shot in blue screen and then composited on top.

Holier Than Thou

The hole in Helen's body is charred and gaping and thoroughly 3-dimensional. It moves as she does, and we can see various parts of the background through it as she turns. Given the hole's dimension and structure, it would seem a natural for 3-D computer graphics. This was not, however, how it was done. For reasons of staffing and speed, Smythe developed a 2-dimensional technique that worked just as well or better. Staff availability also limited the total number of the hole shots that could be done using digital techniques to just over half the total. The rest were completed using optical methods.

In a second effect shot involving Madeline's battered head, a body double for Ms. Streep wears a ten pound appliance that hangs down her back. The double is wearing a blue baggy on her own head so it can later be digitally removed.

A clean plate of the scene has been used to remove the head of the body double.

Once again, the effect started with a couple of motion-control camera passes. After Helen emerges from the fountain, she is steaming mad. Her only desire is to inflict as much or more damage on Madeline as she has received herself. Back in the living room, the two rivals circle each other waiting for an opening to attack.

In the live-action shoot, Hawn was filmed wearing a shirt with a large black circle drawn on it both front and back. The cameras were the same manually-directed motion-control rigs used for Streep's backward-head sequence. Using these cameras, they captured the action and when the live filming was complete, immediately shot a clean plate of the entire sequence with the same camera move.

Cutting Out the Hole

Smythe's team then digitized the live-action shots and used the computer to create mattes from the circles on Hawn's front and back. These mattes were then offset inside the computer by the actual width of Hawn's body.

For the next step, they called up the digitized footage of the clean plate onto the monitor, and the pair of holes were overlayed onto the clean plate, following the motions of Helen's body. Wherever any parts of the two hole mattes overlapped, that was where they could see through the hole to the background of the clean plate. Wherever the holes didn't overlap is where the sides of the body hole were visible.

To create the look of the hole's sides, Smythe had one of his artists create a painting of what he thought it would look like. This image of charred and torn flesh was then overlayed in these nonoverlapping areas to complete the picture. The result was a thoroughly convincing cavity that moved precisely as we might expect, were such a thing possible.

A furious Helen (Goldie Hawn) rises from the fountain to discover a giant hole blown through her middle. ILM used an efficient 2-dimensional computer technique to erase the missing parts of her body.

Finishing Touches

Through careful use of split-screen action, digital painting, body doubles, and shovel handles mounted on invisible filament wires, the reality of the hole was further accentuated. In her fury, Madeline throws a shovel handle at Helen and misses. It passes directly through the hole and stabs into the couch behind.

Most of this effect was accomplished using physical techniques beyond the scope of this book, but it serves to illustrate how the digital and the physical are in an ever-growing collaboration in the quest for believability. Similarly, all of the digital effects of *Death Becomes Her* show that the technology's increasing sophistication is bringing computer graphics into realms not previously open to it.

Index

Index